HOW TO SUCCEED THE BIBLICAL WAY

HOW TO SUCCEED
the
BIBLICAL WAY

RON JENSON

Tyndale House
Publishers, Inc.,
Wheaton, Illinois

Second printing, September 1981

Unless otherwise noted, all Scripture quotations are from the
New American Standard Bible © 1960, 1962, 1963, 1968, 1971 by the Lockman Foundation,
La Habra, CA. Other versions quoted are *The Holy Bible, New International Version* (NIV)
© 1978 by New York International Bible Society; and *The New Testament
in Modern English* © J. B. Phillips, 1958, 1959, 1960, 1972.

LIBRARY OF CONGRESS CATALOG CARD NUMBER 80-54492

ISBN 0-8423-1541-1, PAPER

PRINTED IN THE UNITED STATES OF AMERICA

I dedicate this,
my first book,
to my first love on this earth,
my wife Mary.

CONTENTS

PREFACE

These principles of success have come directly out of the Word of God and from my interaction with people through counseling and teaching over a number of years. God usually communicates truth in the context of relationships and people. Therefore, I want to recognize and thank a few of the people who have helped me to understand and build these principles in my life.

First, my mother and father, Bob and Maxine Jenson, provided the kind of living environment for me to be free to learn the reality of success in my early years. I'm grateful to them.

Second, I want to thank Dr. Bill Bright, the founder and president of Campus Crusade for Christ, who is my boss at this time. He has modeled for me qualities of success in the fullest sense like no man I have ever known before. He taught me that the Holy Spirit is the essential figure in building into my life the qualities I suggest in this book. He is the one who taught me the joy of learning to share my faith with others. He is the one who taught me the life of faith and the need for personal holiness.

Mr. Arthur DeMoss passed away about a year and a half ago. Art taught me that success in the biblical sense, as I have defined it in this book, is a non-negotiable for the Christian. Art

9

had a direct impact on me through his life of faith and his aggressive commitment to reach people for Jesus Christ and the way he lived under God's power and control.

Mr. Robert Safford and Mr. Robert Gladden are two men with whom I had the joy to work in a previous pastorate. These two very successful laymen helped me to think and work through these principles as we shared them together and sought to build them into one anothers' lives. Their friendship and support over the years has been incredibly helpful.

Finally, I want to thank my wife, Mary, who has loved me and supported me for over eleven years. I love her for the way she has allowed me to spend the kind of time and effort that it has taken to work some of these principles out, and to develop them in proper form for communication.

ONE
HOW TO SUCCEED
THE BIBLICAL WAY

Success. For many people the thought of that word brings with it visions of money, homes, cars, popularity, and business advancement. For a Christian, it may be thought of as a word that has no place in his or her life. "I cannot be successful," a Christian may think, "I am to be meek, mild, and unassuming.'

What does God say about success? He wants every Christian to be successful—very successful—even super successful! Jesus was a success at daily living while he was on earth. He succeeded supremely when he overcame death through his resurrection. As a child of the King, a Christian ought to be successful too.

Alexander the Great, we are told, was listening to a young man under trial for misbehavior on the battlefield. The great commander, ready to pardon the young man, asked the young soldier his name. The young man answered, "My name is Alexander, sir." "Alexander?" the leader recoiled in astonishment. "Son, you may have made a mistake in battle, but you have a name to live up to. Either you change your name or change your behavior."

I wonder if God ever feels like that. "Hey, Christian, either change your name or change your behavior. If you are a child of the King, act like it." And that means live successfully. Isn't

11

that what the Lord said to Joshua in charging him to lead Israel into the promised land?

> This book of the law shall not depart from your mouth, but you shall meditate on it day and night, so that you may be careful to do according to all that is written in it for then you will make your way *prosperous,* and then you will have good *success*. [Joshua 1:8, italics mine]

Or, again, consider David's words in Psalm 1:

> How blessed is the man who does not walk in the counsel of the wicked, nor stand in the path of sinners, nor sit in the seat of scoffers! But his delight is in the law of the Lord, and in His law he meditates day and night. And he will be like a tree firmly planted by streams of water, which yields fruit in its season, and its leaf does *not wither;* and in whatever he does he prospers. [Ps. 1:1-3, italics mine]

Fruit, prosperity, success! Doesn't that show that God not only accepts, but delights in and greatly desires, our success? God wants us to be successful.

"Okay, Okay" someone may say, "I can academically accept the fact that God wants me to be successful. But why is it that ungodly people often seem successful while devoted people often seem to fail?"

The answer to that question brings us to another question; "What is success?" Is it the gaining of more money, advancement, or popularity? Christians need to define success. If God wants us to be successful, we should know what it means and how to achieve it.

Biblical success, I believe, is "the *progressive realization* and *internalization* of all that *God wants me* to be and *do*. When we examine that definition carefully, we will see that it has great implications and, if properly understood and applied, it could transform our lives.

12

TWO
GOD WANTS PROGRESS—
NOT PRETENSE

A serious question struck me recently as I was reading a book by Ray Stedman. I asked myself: "Am I progressing in my Christian life or am I pretending?" In his outstanding book, *Authentic Christianity* (Waco, TX: Word, 1977), Stedman made this penetrating statement:

> Because of these elements present in varying degrees at varying times, many new Christians experience intense excitement and joy. The Bible becomes a fresh and exciting book, and meeting with other Christians is a continual joy. The change in their own attitudes and outlook is apparent to everyone, and they find it difficult to understand why they did not become Christians years earlier.
>
> The initial state of euphoria may continue for weeks or even months. But inevitably, sooner or later, the old natural life begins to reassert itself. The glow begins to fade from Christian worship, and Bible reading becomes less and less rewarding. Christian fellowship in meetings and individual contact becomes dull and routine—old habits of thought and action reassert themselves. This is a critical time when one of three possibilities may occur. First, the young Christian continues to decline to the point

of dropping out of all Christian relationships, neglects his Bible totally, has little or no time for prayer, loses interest in spiritual matters entirely, and is finally living no different than he was before he became a Christian. It is true there may be occasional periods of remission with the possibility of eventually establishing a fairly consistent Christian life, but in the majority of cases there is no return at all, at least for many years, and grave doubt is raised as to whether the individual ever became a Christian at all.

The second possibility is that he becomes aware of his cold and rebellious heart, is frightened by the thought of regressing to what he was before, and casts himself in repentance and frustration upon the Lord anew, renewing his trust in God's promises, and perhaps seeking the help of older, more experienced Christians and thereby returning to a state of peace and joy. This cycle may be repeated many times until it becomes the pattern of his experience and he comes to think of it as normal Christianity. On the other hand he may, happily, learn something from each repeated cycle till eventually his eyes are opened to the truth that will deliver him from his rollercoaster experience and he becomes a settled, stable, Spirit-led Christian.

The third and most likely possibility is that the new Christian may discover what millions of others before him have learned: *It is possible to avoid the pain and humiliation of repentance and renewal by maintaining an outward facade of spiritual commitment, moral impeccability, and orthodox behavior*. In doing so he can preserve a reputation for spiritual growth and maturity that is satisfying to the ego and seems to gain much in the way of opportunities for service and the commendation of the Christian community. Such a Christian life style is usually so prevalent around and so little condemned that the new Christian can hardly be blamed for adopting it and regarding it as the expected thing. He drifts into it with scarcely a pang, little

14

realizing that it is a total fraud, a shabby imitation of the real thing. He would be deeply offended if anyone should call him a hypocrite. To him hypocrisy is a deliberate attempt to deceive others, and his own commitment to the doctrine, moral standards, and practice of Christianity is deep and sincere. But in reality he is a hypocrite because the peace he claims to have is present only while his circumstances are untroubled, the joy he sings about never shows on his face, and the love he is forever extolling is reserved only for those who please him. It is all a giant sham, though for the most part an unconscious one. He may be a true Christian in whose heart Christ dwells, but except for rare moments (usually of desperation or high ecstacy) he does not live the Christian life. The quality of life may be moral, often even generous, and it certainly is religious, however it is anything but Christian. Actually it is virtually the same life he lived before receiving Christ, but now it is covered by a thin Christian glaze, a veneer which disappears quickly when events become irritating, difficult, or distressing.

Why do Stedman's words grab us so much? Because they are true. Sometimes we are phonies. Maybe our whole lives are subtle games—no power, just performances. No progress—just pretense. Unconsciously we discern which behavior patterns are essential for Christian respectability in our church or group and then we learn how to live that way. Our group may frown on drinking, smoking, or dancing. So, we do not do those things, or let anyone else know we do, though we may still be grossly sinning in other areas.

I remember consulting some elders in a large church on how to develop their church. One man asked me if, at our church, we allowed our teachers to drink. I said, "I do not know any who do, but we have nothing specific in writing."

He retorted rather strongly, "You mean you would not require those people not to drink?"

I smiled and said, "Dear brother, we would not allow anyone

to be or remain in spiritual leadership who did anything expressly unbiblical like gossip, slander, or acting contentiously." This quieted him and it made the point. God is much more interested in our total life-style than our adherence to a few rules.

Most people don't think their churches are that legalistic. But legalism is a subtle thing. The expected norms for Christian living may be less overt but often they are still real. For example, we may expect our people to always be smiling, carrying their Bibles, being involved in some ministry, or never getting angry. A person can do those things and still just be performing as an actor. God does not want our performance but our progression. Christians are not here on earth to playact a part for other people to see, for that would mean concentrating on the externals. Men look on the outward appearance. But we must concentrate on whether we are growing internally, for "the Lord looks at the heart" (1 Sam. 16:7).

Legalism is subtle. We build imaginary boxes around us with certain behavior expectations as the walls. We think that if only we can live within the box we will succeed. If we step outside the boundary, we don't want to admit it because that would be admitting to failure and we don't want to fail. For instance, if we lose our temper, we won't admit it to ourselves, to others, or to God. We say, "I am not angry; I am just upset." Or, "I am not worried; I am just concerned."

We are afraid to admit failure because of the mistaken idea that to fail makes one a failure. Therefore, it is easier to just act spiritual and live in the box. The family may fight all the way to church and then enter the church looking like spiritual giants. One may have a rotten thought life and yet act pure. The problem is especially difficult for those in Christian leadership, who feel the pressure of people expecting them to behave a certain way. So they succumb and start the pretense. They may seem to have it together but God looks at the heart. And he knows those who are hollow and defeated—those who have made no progress, but just pretense.

"But," one might say, "is there really another way?" You bet! In 2 Corinthians 3 Paul was talking about Moses, who, when he

16

came down out of the mountain after seeing the Lord had to wear a veil over his face. Because he had seen the glory of the Lord it was still reflecting off his face. But later as the glory was departing, he did not want the people to see it so he wore the veil.

In some ways we are like Moses. We have also had one or more mountaintop experiences in our lives. Our experience with the Lord was vital, fresh, and exciting. But, then the glory seemed to depart. There was a lessening of joy, peace, and love. So as not to appear to our friends as "carnal," we put on a veil. We, too, did not want others to see the glory departing. And some of us have been wearing the veil ever since. Paul said:

> Having therefore such a hope, we use great boldness in our speech, and are not as Moses, who used to put a veil over his face that the sons of Israel might not look intently at the end of what was fading away. . . . Now the Lord is the Spirit; and where the Spirit of the Lord is, there is liberty. But we all, with unveiled face beholding as in a mirror the glory of the Lord, are being transformed into the same image from glory to glory, just as from the Lord, the Spirit. [2 Cor. 3:12, 13, 17, 18]

We are not to live in that box, with that facade or veil. We are to rip it off and be progressing—"being transformed into the same image from glory to glory." The Lord's glory should not depart from us, but grow in us.

Paul said the same thing to the young pastor Timothy. "Take pains with these things; be absorbed in them, so that your progress might be evident to all" (1 Tim. 4:15). Timothy, the most visible Christian leader in that area, was not told to look spiritual, but to let all people see his progress. That meant that people would probably know if he was making mistakes and learning from them. Not pretense, but progression.

I remember getting upset with a secretary one time for something she said when she called me at my home. As I rode to the office, I was steaming and rehearsing what words I would use to communicate my feelings. When I got there, I remembered that my "box" forbade anger, so I tried to cover it up. And as I faced her with the anger raging inside of me I tried to act spiritual. I knew I was doing a poor job when she asked if I was angry! In fact, my desire for holding onto my self-concept, which is often directly connected to my "box" image, was so great I started to lie. I first said, "I am not angry." Then it hit me—Jenson, you hypocrite—you phony! "Wait," I said, "I am angry, and I am wrong for that. Please forgive me."

I felt I had lost her respect. But had I? On the contrary. She said, "I appreciate your honesty and I admire you for confessing to me." Wow! She did not reject me. She reaffirmed me. I did not have to pretend to be perfect; I just had to admit my failure and progress.

How does one progress? There is a three-step plan that God has used to teach me how to progress. I use the acrostic C.O.B. to help me remember it.

C—CONFESS

If I am to be progressing in my spiritual life, I must first learn to *confess* my sins as soon as I commit them and fully accept God's forgiveness. That means if I am angry I must admit it to myself and God. God will not cease loving me if I happen to get angry. He simply wants me to admit it.

That is the point of 1 John 1:9 where we are told that, "if we confess our sins God is faithful and righteous to forgive us our sins and to cleanse us from all unrighteousness." God does not say that we are to hate ourselves for an hour or a day and offer penance by being extra good. Rather, we are to admit to God that we are wrong and accept his total forgiveness. God wants us to know by faith that we are justified, which means God regards us just as if we had never sinned.

The writer of Hebrews stated that, "By this will we have been sanctified through the offering of the body of Jesus Christ once for all. And every priest stands daily ministering and offering time after time the same sacrifices, which can never take away sins; but He, having offered one sacrifice for sins for all time, sat down at the right hand of God.... For by one offering He has perfected for all time those who are sanctified.... And their sins and their lawless deeds I will remember no more. Now where there is forgiveness of these things, there is no longer an offering for sin" (Heb. 10:10-12, 17, 18). But somehow we keep trying to offer our own sacrifices for sin.

But we are forgiven. God sees us as clean. We should just accept it! This truth can be graphically illustrated by the chicken farm. Chickens tend to be carnivorous. If one chicken somehow is hurt and starts to bleed and other chickens see the blood, they will peck that bird to death. To alleviate the problem, farmers sometimes paint the windows in the chicken house red. Everything appears red to the chickens because of the filtering process of the red paint, so the blood isn't visible to the other chickens. That is, in a sense, what happened when Jesus died for us. His blood is the filter through which the Father sees us. In other words, the Father does not see our sins. When we confess our sins, we must accept that truth and not let Satan, the deceiver and accuser, condemn us. He delights in making Christians feel guilty, because in that state, they are not usable in God's service.

We need to confess our sins to those we have sinned against. Scripture says that "If therefore you are presenting your offering at the altar, and there remember that your brother has something against you, leave your offering there before the altar, and go your way, first be reconciled to your brother and then come and present your offering" (Matt. 5:23, 24). Jesus was saying that our spiritual relationship is greatly inhibited by discordant human relationships. If we have sinned against someone and have not confessed to that person, we will not be able to experience and claim God's forgiveness until we have.

While in seminary taking a test, I went to the front of the classroom to talk to the professor and happened to glance at someone's paper and saw the answer to one of the questions. I went back to my seat and said to myself, "Should I put down that answer?" I rationalized that I would have put it down anyway, and so I did. A few days later, God greatly convicted me of cheating. I rationalized to myself and to God that one answer on a multiple choice test of 200 questions would not affect my grade but I couldn't clear it with my conscience. Then I promised God that on the next test I would miss one intentionally. But I didn't think God wanted that either. God forced me to admit to myself and to him that I had sinned.

But God would not stop there. He made me go back to my professor, who I knew liked and admired me, and confess. I remember it now as though it happened yesterday. I walked into his office and asked if I could speak to him privately. He was on his way to chapel and wondered if we could talk as we walked. I said, "I do not think so." So we stood there and I did it. I confessed. And I cried.

You know what he did? He started to tell me how much he abhorred what I had done. Of course he didn't! He comforted me, loved me, and told me that he knew other students had cheated many times before but that no one had ever come to him to confess it. He further told me how much he appreciated my honesty and admired my character.

"Admired your character," someone might say, "Why, Jenson, you cheated—you were a cheater." I did cheat, but I confessed it and learned from it. My record was now clean and I was forgiven. Therefore, I was not a cheater—not anymore. Had I not confessed it, I would still be a cheater.

God wants our progress. God loves us even when we cheat. He forgives that. He just wants us to admit it, take off our facade, and accept his love and forgiveness. He does not want our pretense. That is why confession is so critical.

O—OBEY

The second key word to progress in the Christian life is the word *obey*. Once I have confessed my sins I must yield to God totally before he will allow progress. I cannot hold back any area of my life. For instance, sometimes we try to be loving when we are actually bitter. It does not work. It cannot work. God will not let it work. In Colossians 3 Paul used the metaphor of "putting off" certain qualities and "putting on" other qualities. The metaphor was of a man putting off old clothes and putting on new ones.

Imagine a garbage man coming home after work. His clothes are sweaty, dirty, and smelly. He is going out to a formal dinner so he must put on a tuxedo. Instead of taking off his dirty clothes, imagine him putting his tuxedo on over the filthy, smelly ones. "Ridiculous," you say. You are absolutely right. But that is how we live when we try to act spiritual but do not yield ourselves totally to the Lord. God demands more than that we superimpose an outward appearance. God wants us to obey him in putting off the old unrighteous behavior.

B—BELIEVE

The third key word in the progressing life-style is believe. "Without faith it is impossible to please God." That which is not of faith is sin. God delights in our belief. First he wants us to believe that he will live through us. It is the Spirit who allows us to progress from glory to glory. It is the Spirit who produces the fruit of love, joy, peace, gentleness, goodness, kindness, patience, and self-control within us. If we walk in the Spirit, we will produce the fruits of progression.

Once we have confessed our sins to God, accepted his forgiveness, and yielded ourselves totally to him, all we need to do is believe that the God of the universe will live his life through us. That is why Paul prayed that we might know "what is the surpassing greatness of His power toward us who believe" (Eph. 1:19). We literally have the resurrection power of God within us. All we need to do is believe that the Spirit will live that life through us.

I remember when I first embraced this concept. I was told by someone that I was going to go out witnessing with a group of people at a conference I was attending. I told my friend to forget it. I was not going to go out and buttonhole anybody. But my friend said I was and sat me down to go through the *Four Spiritual Laws* booklet. I had never seen this booklet before and only read it over quickly.

About two hundred of us hopped into cars and ended up at the airport. We got out of our cars and everyone started walking up to people witnessing. Not me! I started walking up and down

21

the airport praying that no one would bump into me because I was not planning to bump into anybody. But, it did not work. A friend of mine grabbed me as I was walking by and asked me to talk to the brother of the man to whom he was talking. I was stuck. So, I opened the book and started reading. The guy, a thirty-year-old hippie, started laughing at me. I was upset and asked him to let me finish the book. After a while he stopped laughing and by the time I finished the presentation, he was watery-eyed and told me that he wanted to believe but could not. I did not know how to answer his further questions and help him but, for the first time, I realized that the message had power and God has used me. God used *me!*

I went from this conversation and shared with others that day. I had a new boldness and actually believed that God would empower me. And he did. One young sailor with whom I spoke that day accepted Christ and was obviously touched by the Spirit of God.

God not only empowers us to witness but to minister to believers and to develop character. He can take impatience and transform it into patience, even if it is a thirty-year habit. God's power is made effective in our weakness. The key is that we believe.

God wants us to progress, not to pretend. He wants us to be free. We have not arrived—no one has—but we are progressing. And one day we will be like him. But that will not be until we go to be with the Lord. To pretend to have fully arrived here is heresy.

The key to our progressing is to learn to confess our sins immediately to God, and to man when we have offended someone, and accept God's forgiveness, to obey God in every area of our lives, and to believe that the God of the universe will live his life through us. Then God can begin to show us the freedom of progress in the Christian life.

ASSIGNMENT

1. Keep a diary this week and list all the times during the day that you pretended to be spiritual and really were not. Find

your sin habits and confess them—each time. Accept the forgiveness immediately.

2. Keep a record in your diary of the miracles God does in your life each day. That is right—things that could not be explained apart from the power of the living Christ within you. For example, love where before there was apathy; boldness to share your faith with someone.

3. Meditate for five minutes at a time four times a day, all week on Confessing, Obeying, and Believing (C.O.B.). Think about the implications of these three.

THREE
THE MIND MATTERS

A beginning place for success, once we start to understand it as a progression, is that we realize what God has for us in relation to the way we are to live, what we are to be, and what we are to do. This realization has to do with the way we use our minds.

THE POWER OF MEDITATION

The importance of the mind is demonstrated scripturally as we look at some of the positive results of right thinking and then the negative results or negative influences upon the mind.

Scripture says as a man "thinks within himself, so he is" (Prov. 23:7). Whatever goes into our minds is what we become. It all begins with our thinking.

Someone said, "You sow a thought, you reap an action; you sow an action, you reap a habit; you sow a habit, you reap a character; you sow a character, you reap a destiny." If any of us asks, "What do I want to become?" the key to the answer will be in getting the right data into our minds from the beginning. Because whatever goes into our minds, whether in an intentional way or unintentionally, whether it is through media or any other source, will affect the kind of persons we become. That is why we must begin with the positive step of getting the right things in our minds.

Paul wrote: "Do not be conformed to this world, but be transformed by the renewing of your mind" (Rom. 12:2). The Greek word for "transform" is *metamorphoumai*, from which we get "metamorphosis." The key to becoming what God wants us to be is to get the right things into our minds and then get them into our lives through internalization.

The power of the mind can be seen graphically in three negative influences: *Satan, society,* and *sin. Satan's* number one goal is to keep people out of the kingdom of God—to keep people away from coming to know Christ. But, once he has lost that battle, once we have received Christ, his goal is to immobilize us—to make us useless. The best way to do that is to work in our thoughts and our minds because he knows that what we think about we will become. If he can get junk into our minds, the end result will be junk. Therefore, Satan works specifically and strategically to dull our minds, to lead them in the wrong direction so we start to reflect on the wrong things. Paul wrote: "For our struggle is not against flesh and blood, but against the rulers, against the powers, against the world forces of this darkness, against the spiritual forces of wickedness in the heavenly places" (Eph. 6:12).

Christians struggle with thoughts and attitudes. Satan will constantly try to change the direction of our minds. He will work on impure thoughts and wrong attitudes. He will work on making us bitter—on anything he can to get our minds off track spiritually. If he can do that, he can immobilize us and if he can do that, he can keep us from telling people about the kingdom of God.

Scripture explains how Satan corrupts the mind (2 Cor. 11:3); he defiles the mind (Titus 1:15); he blinds the mind (2 Cor. 4:4); he confuses the mind (2 Cor. 2:11); he unsettles the mind with worry (Luke 12:29); he diverts the mind (James 1:8; 4:8); he discourages the mind (Heb. 12:3). Satan is not only out to destroy the mind. He will also subtly do anything he can to squeeze the influence of Jesus out of our lives. He sometimes does that through another negative influence in our lives— *society.*

Our use of the word *society* refers to the biblical term "world."

26

Romans 12:2 reads, "Do not be conformed to this world [or squeezed into the pattern of the world] but be transformed by the renewing of your mind." Society means all those attitudes, thoughts, and philosophies such as humanism, atheism, existentialism, narcissism (love of self), materialism (love of things), and hedonism (love of pleasure), many of which are communicated through various media. We may have learned them from our parents, our friends, or our teachers at school. Perhaps we learned them from our peer groups (Christian and non-Christian), television, the newspapers, news, movies—almost anything within the world system could be used to communicate the philosophy of Satan. Satan uses these philosophies to dull our senses to the power and majesty of Jesus Christ and his Word.

Gallup Poll findings show that 47 percent of adults over twenty-five claim to have had a religious experience. Most of them claim to be born-again Christians. Yet they seem to make very little impact on our society. One of the reasons for this lack of impact is that Satan has very subtly sucked many of them into the world system. The amount of television being watched today is one indicator. The national average for television viewing is six to eight hours each day according to some researchers. It has been estimated that every person in America is exposed to over five thousand media advertising messages every day in one way or another. By reading the newspaper we subtly pick up hundreds. All of these have an impact on us, overtly and covertly.

Satan used to work in a more subtle way through the world system. He would try to hide the kinds of things he was communicating, because he knew if he went directly to the conscious mind, we would reject it. But today we accept even pornography. A lot of the things that are in movies and on television, that some of us may be watching, are the R rated shows that a couple of years ago would have been X rated. Nudity in the media today is called "sophistication." Others call it dullness to the Spirit of God and the kind of thing that God hates. He hates perversion of the body! He hates eroticism! Yet, we are exposed to it all the time. After a while we tend to become dulled to it.

As Christians, we must realize that we are in warfare and that Satan is trying to use these tools to dull our minds. When we say, "Well, I can live with this—it does not bother me," it might be because we are not grieved by the same kinds of things that grieve God. And the reason that we are not sensitive to the things of the Spirit is because our senses have been dulled. As a part of the world system, we are subject to be affected by it all the time.

Satan overtly uses the world system through television and the media but he also covertly or subtly uses the world system. Two books written by Wilson B. Key in recent years, *Subliminal Seduction* (New York: New American Library, 1974) and *Media Sexploitation* (Englewood Cliffs, NJ: Prentice-Hall, 1976), tell of research of subtle attempts which have been used to influence subliminally the subconscious mind. The attempt of such advertising is to communicate something in a way that the conscious mind cannot pick up, though the subconscious mind can. It has been so powerful on television and in theaters that it has been banned by Congress on television and in movie theaters. But, it still occurs in the kind of media that you and I are exposed to all the time.

Subliminal communication takes some kind of erotic word or symbol and puts it into the advertising so an erotic desire is subconsciously developed within the observer. An example of that can be found in issues of *Newsweek*. One particular advertisement shows a whisky glass with ice cubes in the bottom of it. The temptation is to say, "Well, that is just a photograph," but it often has been painted very carefully. Inside the ice cubes there might be suggestive pictures, symbols, or words carefully drawn in so the conscious mind does not pick it up but the subconscious mind does. The rationale is to produce such an erotic desire within the viewer that he will subconsciously think, "If I drink this whiskey my sexual desires (one of the strongest motivating desires in mankind) will be fulfilled." It is very subtle. I clipped an advertisement out of a Sunday newspaper supplement showing a man smoking a cigarette with the caption, "I will not settle for anything less than taste." On his shoulder, invisible to the conscious mind and casual eye, was the word "sex." The concept communicated was that sexual desires would be fulfilled if one smoked that brand.

We need to realize that we are being manipulated all the time. A spiritual battle is being waged for our minds and the way we respond to this kind of attack is with spiritual warfare. A. W. Tozer talked about the impact of the media: "One way the civilized world destroys men is by preventing them from thinking their own thoughts. Our vastly improved methods of communication, of which the short side boasts so loudly, now enable a few men in strategic centers to feed into millions of minds alien thought stuff ready made and predigested. A little effortless assimilation of these borrowed ideas and the average man has done all the thinking he will or can do. This subtle brainwashing goes on day after day." That is what is happening today. The world system is having a tremendously negative influence upon each one of us in overt and covert forms. We are in spiritual warfare and we need to live like it.

The third negative influence on our minds is *sin*. Satan uses society to influence our sin nature. This sin nature alone is reason enough for us to want to seek God's help in having our minds renewed. And Scripture states clearly that, "the mind set on the flesh is death, but the mind set on the Spirit is life and peace" (Rom. 8:6). The tendency of the natural mind is to be set on the flesh. There is a natural impulse within us to want to be filled with all the philosophies that our world system (under the control of Satan) wants to communicate to us. We are in a battle for our minds and our mind's matter. Satan will do everything in the world he can to get us to be lazy, slothful, and lifeless about getting the right input into our minds. Because we have been flooded with stuff over the years, we have been led down a path that is contrary to the Word of God. We must learn how to fight that battle.

Biblical meditation provides the key to combatting Satan's influence on us through our contacts with the world. Jesus said, as he was talking to the Father in John 17:15, "I do not ask Thee to take them out of the world, but to keep them from the evil one." God is saying to us today that he doesn't want us out of the world. He wants us to be right in the middle of our society, able to deal with the issues through his power. The Lord Jesus also prayed that we would be "kept from the evil one" and had given us all the tools that we needed to be delivered. One of these tools I believe is meditation.

PRODUCT OF MEDITATION

What happens when we meditate? Both Joshua 1:8 and Psalm 1, both of which deal with biblical success, are written in the context of meditation. Joshua 1:8 reads, "This book of the law shall not depart from your mouth, but you shall meditate on it day and night, so that you may be careful to do according to all that is written in it; for then you will make your way prosperous, and then you will have good success." The same concept is found in Psalm 1. The end product of meditation is success and that is what God wants for our lives.

PROCESS OF MEDITATION

Meditation is woven throughout the Old and New Testaments. It is mentioned over and over again, many more times than the biblical concept of quiet time or personal devotions. Christians should have a quiet time. God wants us to have special times alone with him, but the concept of meditation has much more mention in Scripture. Joshua was told to meditate on the Word day and night to have success. Think of that in the light of Satan's use of society to influence us to sin. The Psalmist wrote that the blessed man's delight is in the law of the Lord, and in his law he meditates day and night. The key to prosperity, to success, is meditation upon the Word day and night.

Jesus said, "If you abide in Me and My words abide in you, ask whatever you wish and it shall be done for you. By this is My Father glorified" (John 15:7, 8). Bearing fruit in our prayer life results from abiding in him and his Word abiding in us.

The Lord said, "If you abide in My Word then you are truly disciples of Mine; and you shall know the truth and the truth shall make you free" (John 8:31, 32). This same concept

30

appears in Romans 12:2: "Do not be conformed to this world, but be transformed by the renewing of your mind"; and in Ephesians 4:23: "Be renewed in the spirit of your mind." Colossians 3:16 reads: "Let the Word of Christ richly dwell within you." Paul wrote: "Taking every thought captive to the obedience of Christ" (2 Cor. 10:5).

Peter wrote: "Gird your minds for action" (1 Pet. 1:13). The idea of "girding up the loins of your mind" came from the metaphor of men's dress in those days. Men wore flowing robes with wide belts. When they went to work or to battle, they would reach down, pull the robes up between their legs and fasten them under their belts so they could move about freely. Here is what the Lord is saying through Peter: "Gird up the loins of your mind" (do not allow your mind to flow about freely; you are at warfare and Satan will attack you if your mind flows about.)

It is easy to say, "I can think a wrong thought for a moment. I can handle that. I will not give into it and it will not have an ill effect on me." But, it is that little bit of "flowing about" that Satan will use later. Bringing "every thought captive to the obedience to Christ" (2 Cor. 10:5) through the process of meditation is a nonnegotiable of success.

Basically three words help us define and understand biblical meditation. The first word is *chewing*. The word meditation comes from the idea of rumination as a cow chewing grass. The food goes down into one part of her stomach and later it is regurgitated. The cow chews on it again after it is partly decomposed and she swallows it again. She keeps chewing until it is completely broken down and in a form that can nourish her body. As we meditate on the Word of God over and over, we begin to apply it to parts of our lives until our whole system is nourished.

Our world system pushes us to a "knowledge" mentality as if knowing were the only key. Some Christians can impart all sorts of knowledge. Knowledge is important. It is part of the key. Right thinking is the beginning of right living. But to gain knowledge doesn't mean that we ever apply it. Perhaps we have been to a conference or seminar where we have heard about meditation and could tell someone all about it, but we have never applied it to our own lives. Such knowledge forces us to be proud and puffed up. "Knowledge makes arrogant [puffs up], but love [or knowledge applied] edifies" (1 Cor. 8:1). God wants us to get a lot of facts, to get an understanding, to get a broad grip on the truths about the Christian life. But then we are to take these facts and build them into our lives. That is what meditation can do. We take the concept and meditate upon it, think about it, chew on it, apply it again and again until it infiltrates every area of our lives. Only the Word of God can do it because only the Word of God has the power of the Spirit behind it.

The second word is *analyze*. If we are going to meditate, we need to analyze the passage of Scripture. That means we look at it from every viewpoint. Often we hear something in a cursory way or we read Scripture casually but we really do not analyze what it says.

A doctor was once in a room with his medical students and he said, "Now men and women, I want you to do exactly as I do. Exactly!" He had a bottle with some kind of fluid in it. He took the bottle and said, "Now follow me." They were in a circle, watching him as he stuck one finger in the specimen and then put a finger into his mouth. One by one the students took the bottle, stuck their fingers into it and then into their mouths. Finally, when they were done he said, "Men and women, you were so taken with what I did, you did not analyze—you did not observe. You did not notice that I stuck my forefinger into the specimen bottle and my middle finger into my mouth." The point is, there are sometimes things in our lives that are distracting us from the Word of God and we need to come back to the Bible to see what it really says and not what we think it says.

The third word in defining meditation is to *act upon* it—*obey* it. "This book of the law shall not depart from your mouth but you shall meditate on it day and night, so that you may be careful to do according to all that is written in it" (Josh. 1:8).

We are not talking about Eastern meditation that is based on the concept that man is basically good, and that if we can somehow get everything else out of our minds we will come in contact with a universal omnipresence who is within us so that the best of life will come to the front.

There is validity in some aspects of Eastern meditation. There is value in getting everything out of our minds and just concentrating on nothing. Sometimes good things can happen. Certainly peace can result for at least a short period of time. But, biblical meditation is the absolute opposite of that. Its basis is that man is basically sinful and is therefore in a battle. He has been barraged through society by Satan with all sorts of junk. There has been garbage put in the mind so we need to wash that mind out. The only way to do that is to start pushing the garbage out as we get God's Word into our lives. It does not work just to stop putting junk in or taking all the junk out. All that does is create a vacuum for more garbage. We need to get the Word into our minds, into our hearts, into our actions, into our total beings.

THE PRACTICE OF MEDITATION

There is a physical aspect, a mental aspect, and a repetitive aspect of meditation.

Physical. We do not have to be in any certain kind of position to meditate. We can meditate anytime, anywhere—walking, lying down, sitting, even driving in our cars. It may be good for us to meditate in different positions from time to time.

Mental. An acrostic that is built on the word "MEDITATE" has been helpful to me. There was a time when I needed something to help me, and this acrostic helped me to find a solution.

When I was a young boy, I was constantly getting into trouble. I had a poor self-concept because I was always being called, "Jelly Belly," and I did not like the way I looked. I did not like the person I was. I was so rebellious that I began to internalize my dissatisfaction and became a frustrated, anxious, angry little boy. As a result, I got into fights all the time. That had a lot of implications. I was in trouble with the law for stealing and forgery when I was ten years old. I was in trouble with my family. I was in trouble in school. Every place a kid could get in trouble I did. It was all a manifestation of the problems within me; a poor self-concept and a poor relationship with God. I was a mess. Part of my experience during that time was an exposure to pornography. As a result, my mind was literally filled with rotten thoughts. So as I was growing up as a Christian, even as I got into high school, and on into college, I struggled with my thought life. I had so much junk in my mind that I struggled with it and had trouble purifying my thought life. It became a besetting sin. I had tried to discipline myself, I tried fasting, I tried abstinence from certain things, I tried memorization of Scriptures, I tried having a quiet time, I tried hating myself—I tried everything I could to deal with the problem of my thought life.

The problem became even more acute as I rose to positions of spiritual leadership and I knew that outwardly I had everything in order but internally I was not having victory in a major area of my life. I kept giving in, over and over again. It was a pattern I just could not break. Many of us may not have a problem with thought life. Others may have trouble with their attitudes toward money, or trouble with relationships, some may have problems with bitterness, or worry, or lust for other things. It could be anything. The point is that I had a besetting sin over which I could not get victory.

Then I learned about biblical meditation. I took Colossians 3:1-17 and memorized it thoroughly. After I memorized it, I worked through a process to be explained later. I meditated for a year, four or five times a day, every day, ten to fifteen minutes at a time. God finally worked in me so that my desires to be holy and to think his thoughts were greater than they were to be impure, and to fulfill my desires. I found that I was literally "transformed by the renewing of my mind" (Rom. 12:2). That is what God can do. Some may say, "I have sins in my life, but I just can't get control of them." I am saying that they can get control of them. They need to acquire biblical discipline by learning how to meditate on Scripture.

HOW TO MEDITATE

M—*Memorize*. Choose a passage and memorize it. I took Colossians 3:1-17, which reads, "If then you have been raised up with Christ, keep seeking the things above. . . . set your mind on the things above, not on the things that are on earth. . . ." I memorized it so well I could recite it letter perfect.

E—*Emphasize key words*. Ask, what words do I need to know in this passage. IF I am risen with Christ. Am I risen with Christ or not? What does it mean IF I am risen with Christ? I would write out on a piece of paper, IF. I am RISEN with Christ. What does it mean to be RISEN with Christ? What is the point behind that? SEEK those . . . what does it mean to SEEK? It means to search for, to strive for. I would emphasize key words I wanted to know.

D—*Define them*. Using some different translations of the Bible and a Bible dictionary, I would then define those key words. What do they mean? What does it really mean to seek those things which are above? So often we get such a superficial exposure to the Word of God that we do not understand the meaning behind the words we are reading, so we do not apply them. I need to know what each word means. That does not mean I have to do a lot of in-depth research, but I do need to know the basic meaning.

I—*Individualize*. I said, "Father, I AM risen with your Son. You say I AM sitting at your right hand. I have a resurrection life. Father, since that is true, I AM going to search after and strive for those things that are above." I just kept building that concept within me.

T—*Think about it*. Here I want to visualize each truth. "Father, I am going to seek those things that are above. I am going to search for them." My mind at that point went to Philippians 4:8 which says, "whatever is true, whatever is honorable, whatever is right, whatever is pure, whatever is lovely, whatever is of good repute . . . let your mind dwell on these things."

A—*Apply*. It is one thing for me to say, "I am going to seek those things which are above; I am going to set my affections on things above and not on things on the earth where I am dead and my life is hid with Christ in God." But it is another thing to apply that. So throughout the day when I had opportunity to think a wrong thought, I would say, "Father, since I am risen with you, right now I am going to seek those things that are above." I learned to make it an instant habit pattern response.

T—*Tell others*. Part of meditation, of getting the Word into me is to share it with others. I find every time I get powerful responses from messages I give it is because of illustrations and insights in that message that came right through my own experience. God wants this to happen in our lives. He wants to use us to minister to others as the Word of God is transforming us.

E—*Enjoy the Lord*. We need to let that meditation result in enjoying the Lord. We may possibly have an area in our lives right now that we are struggling with. Then we need to find Scripture related to that area and we need to start building the habit of meditation into our lives. We need to practice it regularly, as often as three or four times a day—when we get up in the morning, when we go to bed, before we fall asleep. Five to ten minutes should be spent on two or three verses just to think about them. If worry is a problem, perhaps Paul's words would be helpful: "Be anxious for nothing, but in everything by prayer and supplication with thanksgiving let your requests be made known to God. And the peace of God . . . shall guard your hearts and minds in Christ Jesus" (Phil. 4:6, 7).

Whatever the area is, remember that Satan's desire is to immobilize and neutralize us by getting us to feel defeated in that area. The only way we are going to have a consistent, ongoing victory is God's way.

36

God's way, among other things, involves being transformed in our life-style; metamorphosed by the renewing of our minds. If we can build this quality into our lives, starting today, and in days to come, we can have consistent victory in every area of our lives. It will take a lot of hard work. We will have to apply some other principles from this book as we go, but we can have consistent victory. No besetting sins should hold us back from having an ongoing impact for eternity.

ASSIGNMENT

1. Memorize the MEDITATION acrostic.
2. Meditate on a passage of Scripture (three or four verses) for ten to twenty minutes, four times a day consistently for the next thirty days.
3. You might want to list key passages for key needs, such as: Love—1 Corinthians 13; Worry—Philippians 4:5-8; Thought Life—Colossians 3:1-17; etc.

FOUR
INTERNALIZATION—
MAKING SUCCESS A HABIT

Success is the progressive realization and *internalization* of all that God wants us to be and do. To internalize the Word of God into our lives we must first get the right data into our minds and hearts through the process of meditation. Then, we need to internalize it so it becomes us—a part of our life-style, a part of our habit pattern. The key for us to remember is the word discipline. God wants us to be disciplined. We make success a habit through discipline—through internalizing the Word of God.

I heard a story about a man who had finished his prison term and entered the free world again. He was having a lot of frustration adapting to free life, and he could not quite understand why. He tried to visualize the struggle he was having by taking a Coke bottle and jamming wires into it. Using large and small wires, he pushed a number of them into the Coke bottle until it broke. After the bottle was broken, the bunched up wires were still intertwined and in the form of a Coke bottle. He then took each wire apart, one by one, and straightened them out. The point of the story is, though he had gotten out of the confines of prison, or his Coke bottle, he still had the habit patterns and attitudes built into him that he had to get straightened out.

The same is true of our lives. When we came to know Jesus Christ, we became legally a free person. Scripture says that right now, positionally, we sit at the right hand of the Father, that we have been forgiven, and that God loves us totally, that he sees us as pure white snow. Yet, we still have within us sinful habit patterns that we have developed from childhood. These habits have been developed and enhanced by the media exploitation of the world system and of Satan's manipulation of it all the time. Though we still have this form of bondage within us, we are legally free. The Spirit-filled life really is the key to the Christian life, but the fruit of the Spirit includes self-control. God's part, according to Philippians 2, is to work in us to give us the will and the power to do his good pleasure. As the Word of God is built into our lives through the power of the Spirit, we begin to want the things that God wants. God gives us new desires. He also gives us the power to experience those desires. Paul wrote that as God works in our desires, we are responsible to work out our own salvation with fear and trembling (Phil. 2:12).

Our job is to be disciplined for the purpose of godliness; to work out what God is working in. There is a balance. As we trust the Holy Spirit, he produces within us the desires God wants and gives us the power to live that way. But, we have to take the initiative to be disciplined so the habit pattern of the Word of God becomes ours.

"Like a city whose walls are broken down is a man who lacks self-control" (Prov. 25:28, NIV). We might have some areas of our lives under self-control, but there might be other areas that we are not aware of, where we do not have self-control. Unless we can get control of our lives in every area, we are easy prey for Satan. When Satan wants to frustrate us or defeat us, he will attack. He can come right into the "city" because there are no walls or fortresses to protect us. God wants us to build up the walls of self-control in every area of our lives so we become what Jesus Christ wants us to become. There is no way to be successful without self-control.

PRINCIPLES OF DISCIPLINE
It is important to recognize what Scripture has to say about discipline. Paul wrote: "Do you not know that those who run in a

race all run, but only one receives the prize? Run in such a way that you may win. And everyone who competes in the games exercises self-control in all things. They then do it to receive a perishable wreath but we an imperishable" (1 Cor. 9:24, 25). When men prepared for the Olympic games during the time when Paul wrote, they went through a very rigorous training program; they maintained very strict diets, very strict exercise programs, very strict sex lives, believing that sexual release resulted in a loss of energy which would hamper their performance—very rigorous self-control.

Paul continued, "Therefore, I run in such a way, as not without aim, I box in such a way as not beating the air" (v. 26). He was very directive in his movement. Paul saw his life as a great athletic event. He moved toward his goal with discipline and very specific direction.

Then he said, "But I buffet my body and make it my slave lest possibly after I have preached to others, I myself should be disqualified" (v. 27). His fear was the disqualification from effectiveness in this life and from reward in eternity. Paul said, "I buffet my body," using a boxing metaphor. In those days boxers tied rawhide with pieces of metal in it around their hands. Paul was saying he would bring every part of his life under control, even if it meant to beat his body black and blue in order to accomplish what God wanted him to accomplish.

There is another principle related to self-control and self-discipline. I also memorized and meditated upon Colossians 3 for a long time. Paul explained the fact that these people had a position with Christ. He said, "You are risen with Christ, you are pure, you are holy." He continued, "Therefore consider the members of your earthly body as dead to immorality, impurity, passion, evil desire, and greed which amounts to idolatry" (3:5). Paul later said, "But now you also, put them all aside: anger, wrath, malice, slander, and abusive speech from your mouth" (3:8). Paul was talking to the same Christians who he described earlier as being already complete in Christ in a positional sense. God says we are perfect, whole, and complete; that we are kings, we are rulers, but we can still live like peasants because we have these habit patterns built into our lives. Paul was saying, "Put them all aside."

The metaphor used earlier, concerning the garbage man who put the tuxedo over his garbage clothes, relates here. We have to put off old clothes before we put on new ones. Part of discipline is learning to put off the old man or put off anger, or put off wrath. Paul said, "And so, as those who have been chosen of God, holy and beloved, put on a heart of compassion, kindness, humility, gentleness, and patience, bearing with one another and forgiving each other" (3:12, 13). These were the very opposite of what he had told them to put off. As we put off something, we put on something.

The Apostle Paul wrote what is probably the classic passage on discipline. "In pointing out these things to the brethren, you will be a good servant of Jesus Christ, constantly nourished on the words of faith and of the sound doctrine which you have been following. But have nothing to do with worldly fables fit only for old women. On the other hand, discipline yourself for the purpose of godliness. For bodily discipline is only of little profit, but godliness is profitable for the life to come" (1 Tim. 4:6-8).

In the context of self-discipline for the purpose of godliness, Paul wrote: "Let no one look down on your youthfulness, but rather in speech, conduct, love, faith and purity show yourself an example of those who believe" (1 Tim. 4:12). Paul was talking to Timothy, a young Christian leader. He told him not to worry about being young in the midst of chronologically older Christians, but he was to be an example among them in love, conduct, faith and purity as well as in speech. The word for discipline in verse 7 in Greek is *gumnazo*, from which we get the word "gymnastics."

I remember watching the summer Olympics a number of years ago. I was specifically watching Nadia Comaneci, who came away with a number of gold medals. I was amazed at her precision. I thought it was easy until I watched a girl practice those same moves at our local YMCA. She came down from the top bar down to the lower bar, spun around and then put her hands back to grab the top bar again. Instead, she went the wrong direction about fifteen feet backwards in the air, landed flat on her back, and hit her head on the floor. I thought, "I bet that happened to Nadia over and over again. I imagine she fell down, stood up, tried it again, fell down, stood up, tried it again. I would guess that pain was involved until the gymnastic move became a habit.

We live in an instant generation—instant coffee, instant breakfast. Everything is instant. Ours is a throwaway generation. If it doesn't work, we just throw it away; we do not fix it. That attitude has pervaded our mentality so much as Christians that unless we become instantly spiritual in every area of our lives, unless we get immediate victory over sin habits in our lives, we become frustrated, defeated, and want to give up. The key to discipline is *gumnazo*, exercising ourselves for godliness; trying over and over again until God's habits become our habits. As the Spirit of God works in us, we work those things out by constant repetition.

Paul wrote again to Timothy:

> You therefore, my son, be strong in the grace that is in Christ Jesus.... Suffer hardship with me, as a good soldier of Christ. No soldier in active service entangles himself in the affairs of everyday life, so that he may please the one who enlisted him as a soldier. And also if any one competes as an athlete, he does not win the prize unless he competes according to the rules. The hardworking farmer ought to be the first to receive his share of his crops. [2 Tim. 2:1, 3-6]

Paul spoke of pain and concentration. Later he wrote: "I suffer hardship even to imprisonment as a criminal; but the Word of God is not imprisoned. For this reason I endure all things for the sake of those who are chosen" (2 Tim. 2:9, 10).

The author of Hebrews mentioned the need for discipline:

Concerning him we have much to say and it is hard to explain since you have become dull of hearing. For though by this time you ought to be teachers, you have need again for some one to teach you the elementary principles of the oracles of God, and you have come to need milk and not solid food. For everyone who partakes only of milk is not accustomed to the word of righteousness for he is a babe. But solid food is for the mature, who because of practice have their senses trained to discern good and evil. [Heb. 5:11-14]

He said they had not disciplined their thought life. And as a result, they needed to be treated like little babes, who need to start with baby food and milk and infant training all over again.

In Hebrews 12, the author was talking about the Christians being motivated to a life of commitment and he used the Lord's illustration:

Therefore, since we have so great a cloud of witnesses surrounding us, let us also lay aside every encumbrance and the sin which so easily entangles us, and let us run with endurance the race that is set before us, fixing our eyes on Jesus, the author and perfecter of faith, who for the joy set before Him endured the cross, despising the shame, and has sat down at the right hand of the throne of God. For consider Him who has endured such hostility by sinners against Himself, so that you may not grow weary and lose heart. You have not yet resisted to the point of shedding blood in your striving against sin. [Heb. 12:1-4]

God has given us a very clear-cut and practical theology of discipline. It is a nonnegotiable in the Christian life. If we do not build the habit of discipline into our lives starting now, we can never be totally what God wants us to be. God wants us to be successful. Certain principles are related to discipline.

SACRIFICE

Paul said it was important that we have self-control or sacrifice (1 Cor. 9). Paul talked about suffering hardship as a soldier (2 Tim. 2). We have to pay the price to be disciplined. We have to sacrifice.

PAIN

Discipline, self-discipline, and self-control involve pain. Paul said, "I buffet my body. I beat it black and blue." Hebrews 12 reads, "You have not yet resisted to the point of shedding blood in your striving against sin." There is pain in self-discipline. There is no way we can be a great athlete without being willing to face and move through the pain barrier. If we are going to be a great runner, we must learn to live with pain. Any athlete who is going to exercise himself for the purpose of success has to pay the price in pain.

In high school I played football, tennis, and a number of other sports. In every sport I had to pay the price in pain, but for what I wanted to achieve; it was worth it. If we are going to be disciplined men and women of God, we must be willing to suffer pain. Just because we try a couple of times to deal with worry and it becomes painful, we cannot give up.

CONCENTRATION

To be disciplined, we need to take one area of our lives at a time and concentrate on it. Concentrate. Zero in on it and work on one area at a time.

REPETITION

We need to keep doing it over and over again. We are told that it takes sixty days of successful practice of one activity before it becomes a habit. The goal of discipline is to develop godly habits. That means, if we are having trouble in our thought life, we must build the Word of God into our lives and practice forty-five to sixty consistent days of right thinking before that habit will be developed into our lives. God wants that habit there so he can develop walls that can handle satanic attack.

HABIT

It needs to become a habit. Something is a habit when we do it instinctively and without thinking about doing it. We all have habits. Which way do we button our shirts or blouses—from the bottom up or the top down? Some of us have to look at our shirts because we do not remember. It has become a habit. When we brush our teeth, how do we squeeze the tooth paste? We do not think about these things, because they have become habits. The Bible teaches that we are to put off the old man and to put on the new man, so that godliness becomes a habit. The way we build habits into our lives is through constant, ongoing repetition. Each one of the Scriptures mentioned above relates to holy habits. We must keep putting off the old man and putting on the new man over and over again, day after day, until it becomes a life-style.

I was in a Sears store one day years ago with a friend of mine. As we were walking along I said something to him. He turned to me and spit in my face. (This is a true story.) Being a Christian gentleman and not wanting to demonstrate my anger, I just took out my handkerchief and wiped my face. I didn't say anything. I thought, "He will feel guilty and will say something about it." But he didn't say anything.

We kept walking along and I spoke to him again. We were laughing about something, with people all around us, and this guy turned and spit in my face again. I took my handkerchief out again and wiped my face. I thought, "This guy is really crazy. I cannot believe it!" I expected him to say something to me but he didn't. He just smiled and gave me a stupid look as we were walking.

Well, he looked at me a third time and spit in my face. What would you do in that situation? Do you know what I did? I did not do anything. He was my two-month-old son!

Someone might say, on hearing the first part of that story, "That's horrible! Why would a person do that?" But when they learn that it is a two-month-old child, they might say, "Big deal. A baby will learn not to do things like that." Of course, that kind of behavior is expected from a child.

But think how God feels. Some of us have been Christians for quite a while and yet we are beset with the kinds of sins one would expect from a new Christian. I know that for a fact, because I have struggled with some of those sin habits myself, the kind over which many Christians have not yet gotten the victory. Some of us have not gotten victory over our anger, or our worry, or our desire for material things, or our thought life, or our eating habits, or our physical discipline habits, or a number of other habits. We have not gotten control over our tongues. Perhaps God is saying to us "When you were a new Christian I could understand that, but now that you are growing as a Christian, there are more years behind you and you understand some biblical principles. It is abhorrent to me that you would not be disciplined in that area." I really believe God would want us to know that. God wants us to have ongoing victory in every area of our lives, with no hidden areas of indiscipline.

PRACTICES OF DISCIPLINE

Discern the problem. We should determine what the problem is in our lives. It may be something we are doing that we should not do, or it could be something that we are not doing that we should do. Let us imagine the problem is worry. Step one is to discern and label the problem as worry. We shouldn't say, "I am not worried; I am just concerned. Everybody is concerned today. My family is concerned, everybody I know worries a little bit." We shouldn't rationalize but say, "This is a problem. It is sin. It is wrong."

Discover the biblical alternative. Scripture tells us to put off the old man and put on the new man. "Put off anger, wrath, malice. Put on love, a heart of compassion, forgiveness" (Col. 3). Finding the biblical alternative is putting on the opposite of what we have put off. The opposite of worry is trust. Instead of worrying about things, we must follow the advice of our Lord. "Look at the birds of the air, that they do not sow, neither do they reap, nor gather into barns, and yet your heavenly Father

47

feeds them. Are you not worth much more than they?... Observe how the lilies of the field grow; they do not toil nor do they spin.... But if God so arrays the grass of the field, which is alive today and tomorrow is thrown into the furnace, will He not much more do so for you?" (Matt. 6:26, 28, 30) Paul wrote: "Be anxious for nothing, but in everything by prayer and supplication with thanksgiving let your requests be made known to God. And the peace of God, which surpasses all comprehension, shall guard your hearts and minds in Christ Jesus" (Phil. 4:6, 7). In Psalm 37 there is a pattern of seven things that we should do to deal with worry. The first statement is, "Fret not ..." And then once we have identified worry, and have "put it off," we find the biblical alternative, which is, in this case, trust in the Lord. Commit your way unto the Lord, delight yourself in the Lord, rest in the Lord, wait on the Lord. We have got to do those things when we put off an activity.

Develop the whole situation for change. Life is like a cycle. At different times, different things stimulate sin responses out of habit. Perhaps we have grown up conditioned to worry if we find ourselves in certain settings, and we start to worry out of habit. When we "put off" something like worry, we must put something in its place or that void will be filled with worry again.

We can say, "Okay, I am not going to worry. I am going to stop worrying." But we have to restructure the whole situation and say, "Father, instead of worrying, I am going to dwell on the positive things you want me to put into my mind." Instead of worrying, Scripture says, "Fret not.... Trust in the Lord." We must say, "All right, Father, I trust you. I commit my way to you. Lord, I yield my life to you and you have absolute control of it."

Instead of worrying, we must spend a good deal of time meditating on Scripture and delighting ourselves in the Lord at that given moment. We must sing songs back to him and respond to him and praise and adore him. Then Scripture says, "Rest in the Lord." "Father, I am just going to rest in you." And then "wait on the Lord." "Father I am going to wait eagerly for you to show me your will."

If we can build these principles into our lives and restructure the whole situation so that when we are tempted we immediately put off that sin and put on the other attitude, we start to develop a habit. But we must do it over and over again until it becomes a habit. When we have developed a new habit pattern, our immediate response will be rejoicing and trusting.

I grew up with a terrible habit of impatience and anger. I used to get into fights all the way through school. Now, I believe one of the strengths of my life is patience; a habit God has built into my life as I followed the above procedure. God's strength was made perfect in my weakness. That is what he wants to do in all of our lives.

Disconnect the chain of sin. We want to stop worrying and activate the right kind of life-style. We want to put off the old man and put on the new man. If we do not get on top of some of our sin habits now, if there is a habit in our lives over which we haven't gotten victory, we cannot maintain any degree of spirituality in our lives. We will fall asleep as Christians. We will become dulled to the Christian life. When a person falls asleep spiritually,

1. He will not realize he is asleep. He will be unaware of what is going on in the spiritual world.

2. When he sleeps, he dreams of things to do that he would do if he were awake. If he is asleep spiritually, he starts to think about things to do that are wrong and improper; things he would not do if he were spiritually awake.

3. He doesn't want to be awakened once he is asleep. He does not want people to point out the fact that there might be an area in his life that he is unaware of. He doesn't want to be made aware of areas in his life that he might have to deal with.

4. He is unaware of what is going on around him when he is asleep. Because he is unaware of what is around him, he is insensitive to needs of himself or others.

5. He becomes a mass of contradictions because the way he is living outwardly is not true of the way he is living inwardly. Frustration develops.

6. Finally if these things continue, the Christian often becomes desperate to the point of death. He either gives up the Christian life or gives up his physical life. The problem is that he is not able to go on top of sin habits that run through his life.

Depend on help from others. We cannot be disciplined without the help of others. I remember one time I was meeting with a group of people with whom I was developing a singles ministry at our church in Philadelphia. I said to them, "I want all of us to have specific goals and objectives to develop a godly life-style. I sense that I need to lose weight."

One of the new Christians who did not know any better said, "Do you really want to lose weight?"

I said, "Yes."

He answered, "How about every week when we get together on Thursday night, we bring some scales down here and put you on them.

I said, "Well, I . . . I do not know if I want to lose weight that much."

He said, "No, that is the way to do it." So every Thursday night, he would bring the scales and put them right in front of me. I would have to get on and weigh in. Do you know what that did to me? It created a lot of desires in me. Because of the accountability to the group, whenever we would meet on Thursday night, I would think, "Maybe I ought to set the dial back so it looks like I lost weight. Or maybe I ought to tell them that the scales are broken." All that temptation came because of the pressure of accountability. That is what God wants, the pressure of accountability. We should get some friends to help us in areas where we are weak.

Dwell on your whole relationship to Christ. I am convinced that if we are not disciplined in our minds, we will have difficulty in other areas. Obesity, in my book, is as hard to change because it is a life-style, as any habit I know. Obesity and overeating usually spring forth from problems people have had with self-concept or with anger or with nervousness. Until they can deal with the root problems, it is hard to change. But it can be done! The key is that every part of our lives is important. Our physical lives and the way we eat, the way we exercise, has a direct relationship to the control of our tongues, the control of our attitudes, and thoughts.

Drill the new pattern into your life. We must make a habit of the new pattern. We don't become godly in an instant. We need to keep putting off the old area and putting on the Word of God, meditating upon the Word of God, every day, three or four times a day, until it becomes a habit pattern.

THE PRODUCT OF DISCIPLINE

Paul wrote "In speech, conduct, love, faith, and purity, show yourself an example of those who believe" (1 Tim. 4:12). The place we begin discipline is to ask: "Am I disciplined in the area of my speech, my tongue? Am I disciplined in the area of my conduct? Am I disciplined in the area of love? Do I really love people? Am I disciplined in the area of faith? Am I disciplined in the area of purity? Am I really pure or do I act outwardly different than my thought life?"

Scripture says everyone that looks on a woman to lust for her has committed adultery with her already in his heart. (Matt. 5:28). God knows everything that is going on within us. He knows every crummy attitude and thought. He is aware of it, even though we might fool others. God wants us to be disciplined in purity. He wants us to be holy.

God is interested that we demonstrate ourselves as examples in speech, conduct, love, faith, and purity. Speech is the first one. I believe the reason for that is given in James 3. We are told that anyone who can control the tongue can control his whole life. The tongue is potentially the most devastating and powerful part of the human body. Scripture says in James that the tongue is like a rudder of a ship; a tiny little rudder that gives direction to the whole ship. It is like the bit in the mouth of a horse—a very small piece of metal, but it can direct the horse. The tongue is a powerful tool. And God wants us to be able to discipline it.

Paul gave us the qualities for a disciplined tongue in three questions. Anything we say ought to fit in these three categories. Question one: *Is what we say true?* "Therefore, laying aside falsehood, speak truth, each one of you to his neighbor" (Eph. 4:25). There is always a tremendous tendency to exaggerate or even to lie, but God hates it.

The second question is, *is it kind?* "Let all bitterness and wrath and anger and clamor and slander be put away from you" (4:31). Slander is telling something about someone else, even if it is true, that demeans the character of that person. God hates that. Is what we are saying kind? "Be kind to one another, tender-hearted" (4:32). My words ought to be kind. I ought to ask whenever I speak, "Lord, is this a kind thing to say?"

The third question, *is it necessary?* "Let no unwholesome word proceed from your mouth, but only such a word as is good for edification according to the need of the moment, that it may give grace to those who hear" (Eph. 4:29). When we speak, we need to speak so that we meet the needs of a person at a particular moment.

We need to learn to discipline our tongues so when we speak, we test it with the questions: "Is it true? Is it kind? Is it necessary?"

The tongue is a good place to begin. We must look at our lives and say, "Lord, what one area is the greatest besetting sin or unholy habit I have?" When we start to work through these principles, we will be well on our way to realizing and internalizing what God wants us to do and be.

ASSIGNMENT

1. Isolate in your mind *one* besetting sin.
2. Follow the steps in the Practice of Discipline section for forty days in a row.
3. Keep a daily log of your progress.

FIVE
WHO RULES OUR LIVES?

Success, we have said, is the *progressive realization* (what I know) *and internalization* (what I become) *of all that God wants me to be and do*. The next step in success is to become *all that God wants*. The Lordship of Christ must become a reality in our lives.

What does it mean that we are becoming and doing all that God wants? First, we need to understand the biblical basis for the Lordship of Christ in our lives. Second, we need to understand what the manifestations of the Lordship of Christ in a Christian's life will be.

THE BIBLICAL BASIS
Jesus said, "He who has My commandments, and keeps them, he it is who loves Me, and he who loves Me will be loved by My Father, and I will love him and I will disclose Myself to him" (John 14:21). Keeping his commandments is a prerequisite to the manifestation of Christ in our lives. Paul wrote: "Do not be conformed to this world, but be transformed by the renewing of your mind" (Rom. 12:2). Earlier Paul said, "I urge you therefore, brethren, by the mercies of God, to present your bodies a living and holy sacrifice, acceptable to God" (Rom. 12:1). The

phrase, "present your bodies," is in the aorist tense in the Greek, which denotes a one-time act. In one sense, we daily yield ourselves over and over again to the Lord, and we reckon ourselves dead unto sin and alive unto God. There is a very logical relationship between Romans chapters 1—11 and Paul's statement in chapter 12.

Paraphrased, the first two verses of Romans 12 might read: "Therefore, based on all I have said before, I beseech you—I beg you to present your body a living sacrifice." I think Paul was saying that once and for all, now that we have understood the principles of the Christian life, we should give our lives wholly, irrevocably, to God, never looking back again, and from this point on, follow him. We will sin—we will blow it, we will make mistakes, but we must keep pressing on into the likeness of Christ.

The Great Commission in Matthew 28 says, in essence, that the job of every Christian is to make disciples of all nations. We do this by baptizing them in the name of the Father, and the Son, and the Holy Spirit. The biblical point of baptism is that we identify them with the body of Christ and a local church family.

People are not only made disciples by baptizing them but by "teaching them to observe all that [Christ has] commanded" (v. 20). The end product of belief is obeying him in all things. The bottom line of making disciples is developing men and women who are totally and unconditionally committed to obey everything God has said. Christ wants to be Lord of the entire life and that is part of the process of making disciples. That is at the heart of the biblical mandate. It is not enough to share Christ with people and see them accept him. We must see them absorbed into a body of believers and becoming obedient to all that God wants so that the body of Christ has an influence on our society.

God does not want us to stop there. He wants us to press on, seeing people become committed, reproducing believers. The key to that is that we become the kind of disciples who manifest the Lordship of Christ in our own lives.

54

SPECIFIC MANIFESTATIONS OF CHRIST'S LORDSHIP

The word "disciple" appears 268 times in the New Testament and is used in three distinct ways. One kind we might call *professing disciples*. The five thousand who followed Christ around may have claimed to be disciples in the sense that they were following a teacher. They were mostly just curious observers.

A second type we might call *possessing disciples*. They became convinced academically of what Christ said and they became believers as we would understand believers today. They were called possessing disciples because the Holy Spirit came to indwell their lives, after the death of Christ and the coming of the Holy Spirit to the Church.

The third type of disciple we might call *progressing disciples*. A progressive disciple is a believer who is committed. Progressing disciples are not only curious and professing, they are not only possessing the Holy Spirit and convinced academically about Christ, but they are committed people. That is the kind of disciple the Lord wants us to be. The Lord said to those who had believed, "Now if you continue in My Word then you are My disciples indeed. And you shall know the Truth and the Truth shall set you free" (John 8:30, 31).

Certain qualities or manifestations of the progressing disciple that the Lord taught are true today for a progressing disciple in order to successfully live under the Lordship of Christ on a day-to-day basis.

Christ-centered love. Jesus said, "If anyone comes to Me and does not hate his own father and mother and wife and children and brothers and sisters, yes, and even his own life, he cannot be my disciple" (Luke 14:26). Does this mean we are to hate our brothers, sisters, mothers, or fathers? Obviously not, for Scripture in other places tells us we are to love and obey our parents. God has commanded men to love their wives the way Christ loved the church and to love and care for children and to bring them up in the nurture and admonition of the Lord. Are we to hate ourselves? No, for to have a healthy self-love and respect is what God desires for us. We are to appreciate the fact that, though we are sinful, God has made us in his image and has given us unique gifts so that we are all special children of the King.

"Then what does this verse mean?" someone may ask. Jesus was saying that, in comparison to our love for all of these, our love for Jesus Christ ought to be so supreme, so overwhelming, that the other love seems as hate by comparison. God wants a supreme, supernatural, Christ-centered love on the part of Christians.

What would Christ-centered love look like? The Apostle Paul is a good example. Paul was known as Saul before he became an apostle. He was commissioned to help stamp out the Christian sect, or cult, that he conceived was anti-God. He was responsible for the persecution of many Christians and the death of at least one—Stephen. Then Paul had an experience with the Lord on the road to Damascus. Following that tremendous conversion experience, he went away to "seminary" for a couple of years, probably to some kind of refuge in the region of Sinai, where God retaught him, rubbed off his rough edges, and developed within Paul a supreme love for Jesus Christ.

Paul later wrote: "If anyone else has a mind to put confidence in the flesh, I far more: circumcised the eighth day, of the nation of Israel, of the tribe of Benjamin, as to zeal, a persecutor of the church, as to the righteousness which is of the Law, found blameless." That expression meant that he kept every one of these laws outwardly. He was considered a holy, righteous man in the eyes of others. "But whatever things were gain to me, those things I have counted as loss for the sake of Christ. More than that, I count all things to be loss in view of the surpassing value of knowing Christ Jesus my Lord, for whom I have suffered the loss of all things" (Phil. 3:4-8). That meant loss of reputation, loss of background, rejection by his family, the religious world, the political world, his social world. Everything that was meaningful to him he said, because of his love for Christ, he counted it as loss. "And count them but rubbish in order that I might gain Christ, and may be found in Him" (vv. 8, 9).

When Paul was rethinking his new life in Christ, he made a conscious, intellectual, volitional decision to say that Jesus Christ was the ruler of the world. He did come out of the grave; he is the King; he is the only Truth and without him men will die and go to hell. Therefore his decision was to follow him totally and irrevocably. Everything else was going to be immaterial to his love and devotion to Christ. That is what Scripture really asks Christians to become—totally and absolutely committed to Christ.

A. W. Tozer is one of the most godly men and authors of recent history. He asked certain questions which will give us an indication where our supreme love might be. "What do I want the most? When everything is gone, when all the activities you have to do are done, when you are alone, what do you want more than anything else in the world?" I believe Scripture tells us that it ought to be to know him; to know Christ in a personal, intimate way. "What do you really want the most?"

The second question is, "What do I think about the most?" We have to think about a lot of things—school, ministry, family, job. But when we are alone, what is the thing that secretly occupies our minds. Is it our reputation, the future, power, money, the Lord, or the ministry? It is a good question to ask ourselves.

The third question is "How do I spend my money?" We might spend it on a lot of things. We might tithe (give a tenth of what we earn to the Lord), but whatever we have left, how do we spend it?

Another question is, "What do I do with my leisure time?" Everyone is busy but, when we have that time to be alone, how do we spend it? Is it watching TV, listening to the radio, reading, or sports? How does that activity demonstrate our supreme love?

Another question is, "What kind of company do I enjoy?" If we could be with anybody, with whom would we want to be with and why?

Then a final question is, "Whom and what do I admire the most?" What things in life do we admire the most? Is it the qualities of Christ or people who represent the qualities of Christ, or is it people who might have made a powerful impact in the business or professional world? God knows there are a lot of good principles in the business world and God is often using laymen in full-time secular work. Praise God for that. But there are things in Christ that ought to be admired even more.

A good illustration of what I am talking about is demonstrated in the following:

> A zealous man in religion is pre-eminently a man of one thing. It is not enough to say that he is earnest, hardy and uncompromising, thoroughgoing, wholehearted, fervent in spirit. He only sees one thing, he cares for one thing, he lives for one thing, he is swallowed up in one thing and that one thing is to please God. Whether he lives or whether he dies, whether he has health or whether he has sickness, whether he is rich or whether he is poor, whether he pleases man or whether he gives offense, whether he is thought wise or whether he is thought foolish, whether he gets blame or whether he gets shame, for all this a zealous man cares nothing at all. He burns for one thing and that one thing is to please God and to advance God's glory. [Bishop Ryle. *Practical Religion* (London: James Clark & Co., Ltd, 1959]

God wants men and women who burn for one thing. That may sound fanatical. It is totally inconsistent with natural thinking, but I believe we are so influenced by the world system that it may take that kind of fanatical living to have any impact on our day—people who are totally, irrevocably given over to the Lordship of Christ in their lives. Such a life will demonstrate in reality a Christ-centered love.

Compassion for the brethren. In John 17, Jesus prayed for those the Father had given him out of the world in order that they might be one. Later on he asked, "that they also may be in us that the world might know that Thou didst send me" (17:21). The greatest evangelistic impact the body of Christ will ever have is to manifest a supernatural love toward one another. If believers are radically loving one another, then non-Christians who are suffering from dehumanization and depersonalization see that and will say, "Whatever those people have, I want."

When I was in college, our fellowship group saw the homecoming queen, the president of the student body, the quarterback of the football team, and number of other people come up, one by one, and say to us, "Whatever you people have, I want." It was not just because we were living exciting vivacious, committed Christian lives personally, though that was part of it. They were attracted because whenever we got together they saw a supernatural love and unity. There was no backbiting, no griping or complaining. We cared for one another. We demonstrated a love relationship and a commitment to one another. When they saw that they said, "I do not see that anywhere else and whatever you have, I want." As a result, they accepted Jesus Christ because they saw he was the person who made that possible. Love is a powerful attracting tool.

That kind of love is demonstrated in John 13:35: "By this all men will know that you are My disciples, if you have love for one another."

If you have great faith? No. If you have a tremendous evangelistic zeal? No. If you are tremendously obedient? No. All of these are important, but people will know that we are his disciples if we love one another.

Crucifixion of self. Jesus said, "If any man wishes to come after me, let him deny himself, and take up his cross, and follow Me" (Matt. 16:24). Denial of self is simply saying no to self on a daily basis. One of the qualities of a person under the lordship of Christ is crucifixion of self. Such a life is totally and consistently yielded to the Lord Jesus Christ in all that is done and said. Self-denial is illustrated by a letter that was written by a young convert to communism. Communism began in 1903 with seventeen followers. Today it is threatening to engulf the world, although the mass of people in communist countries are not communist in the purest sense of that term. It is because a few people have been so radically committed to communism and denied themselves in the process, that they have made communism spread. Here is what he wrote to his fiancée:

> There is one thing in which I am dead earnest about and that is the communist cause. It is my life, my business, my hobby, my sweetheart, my wife and mistress, my breath and my meat. I work at it at the day time and dream of it at night. Its hold on me grows, not lessens as time goes on. Therefore, I cannot carry on a friendship, a love affair, or even a conversation without relating it to this force which both thrives and guides my life. I evaluate people, books, ideas and actions according to how they affect the communist cause and by their attitude toward it. I have already been in jail because of my ideals and if necessary I am ready to go before a firing squad.

Choosing the cross. Again in Matthew 16:24 we read: "If any man wishes to come after Me, let him deny himself, take up his cross and follow Me." Peter wrote that we should not be surprised when we suffer as Christians (1 Pet. 4:12).

We do not suffer physically today like people in many parts of the world. A student in our seminary is named Ratha. Ratha was led to Christ by a couple who directed the Campus Crusade for Christ ministry in Cambodia and stayed there after the overthrow by the Khmer Rouge. Ratha watched people being massacred left and right. Hundreds of thousands of people were killed in that siege.

People are still being killed in Cambodia today, being starved to death by inhumane practices that ought to infuriate all of us. Ratha finally made his way out of the country, but he led over fifty people to Christ in the process. He has told us about some of the atrocities, some of them happening there still at the time of the writing of this book. We in this country haven't experienced suffering like that, but the Bible says that as Christians, we may have to go through suffering someday.

Paul wrote "Those who desire to live godly in Christ Jesus shall suffer persecution" (2 Tim. 3:12). I have never suffered the kind of physical persecution as the Cambodians have. I do believe that such suffering is a possibility in our lifetime, even in America. But there are other kinds of suffering that we can expect to face. While in college, as a new Christian, I had just been trained how to share my faith. I was as bold as a lion and I saw some people come to Christ. A couple of friends came to me after a while—Christian friends—and said, "Ron, you are too aggressive. You are very offensive. You are turning people off because you are pushy."

I didn't think I was pushy, although I knew I was being aggressive. I thought I was loving enough to know how to do it. But, when they said that, my desire to be loved and accepted by them was so great that I turned inward and asked, "God, am I too pushy, am I unkind? I don't want to be offensive." I totally retreated as a Christian and stopped reached out to people altogether.

The cross of Christ is going to offend people. God forgive us if we are not bold enough, if we stop communicating the message of the cross because it is offensive to some. Paul said, when he preached the gospel to some he was a sweet odor of life to life and to some a stench to death. People hated Paul. They were either hot or cold toward him.

Being offensive is not fashionable today. I believe we ought to be polite, courteous, and gracious. I do not believe we have to have people spitting in our faces. What we need to do as Christians, is to have a strong emphasis upon the reality of Christ in our lives and not be afraid if some people reject us, because rejecting us is really rejecting the cross. If they reject us because our personalities are offensive, God forgive us for that. But God forbid if we are not bold enough by the power of the Spirit to proclaim the gospel. The cross of Christ offends people because it reminds them that they are sinners and will have to die.

I had retreated for about five months when God said to me, "Ron, you are going to have to make a decision. You are either going to be here on earth to please me or to please your friends. I want you to listen to criticism, but I don't want you to react to them, to respond in an offensive way, but I do want you to ask me if you should change or continue. But do not retreat because some people do not like your approach."

As a result I developed some convictions. This revolutionized my life. I said, "God, I am willing to pick up the cross."

Some people have told me that their husband or wife is their cross, but the cross is not a person or thing in our lives. The cross is a path of dishonor and reproach, something typified in the cross of Christ. As Christians we are going to receive dishonor and reproach. Some people will love us but some are not going to like us because of our principles and because of the gospel we preach. We must make a volitional decision that we are willing to accept rejection.

To me the most important thing in the world used to be that people liked Ron Jenson. I was the student body president, and in front of our student body over seventy-five times. The boldest witness I had all the way through high school was to quote a little bit from 1 Corinthians 13 in my graduation speech. I thought that was being bold, but I had not been trained to do anything else. I went back to a ten-year reunion of my class and learned that some of the people in my class had committed murder and suicide, people were divorced, defeated, and frustrated. I said, "Oh, Lord, if only I had loved them enough and known enough then to be able to communicate the gospel to them. I wish I had been honest and open and not cared if everybody did not remember me.

When I graduated from high school I was voted "most likely to be remembered." That was a great honor, but when I got into college and started in the ministry, I realized that if people just remember Ron Jenson as the nice guy, what have I accomplished in life? I do not want to be offensive, but if I am afraid to be bold because of my reputation, I must come to the place where I am willing to take up my cross every day and place my reputation in God's hands.

Chasing after Christ. Jesus said, "If any man would come after Me, let him deny himself, take up his cross and follow me" (Matt. 16:24). Christ was talking about a continual, ongoing, volitional, and knowledgeable decision to follow him and live the way he wants us to live. Scripture says, "No one after putting his hand to the plow and looking back, is fit for the kingdom of God" (Luke 9:62). The idea is that as Christians, we must make the decision to follow Christ and every day, for the rest of our lives, follow him.

Some may feel that the Christian life ought to be more emotional. God wants us to have joy and peace, but emotion is not at the heart of the Christian life. When I accepted Christ at a retreat I had a tremendous emotional experience. I read my Bible and prayed for a couple of days, but the emotional part fizzled out. I went back to another retreat, got very excited and turned on, went home and read my Bible again and then blew it again. I accepted Christ thirteen times until I came to the realization that once I had accepted him, he came into my life, and would never leave me nor forsake me. Christ had not left me—I was just not experiencing his love in my life. What I had been seeking was only an emotional experience.

I am all for emotions. I believe as Christians we ought to know how to experience emotional worship, but God works through our minds and our wills, and our emotions come as a result. The emotions God wants us to experience in our lives are love, joy, and peace. I do not have to get up in the morning and say, "Wow! It is so great to be a Christian!" I am just not build that way.

We shouldn't feel that if our emotions fall through the cracks, that we are not committed Christians. Emotions are not what God is looking for. Emotions will come. Following Christ means that we continue to be with him, regardless of how we feel.

63

Continuance in the Word. Another of the qualities of a committed disciple, someone under the lordship of Christ, is that of continuing in the Word so that it controls every area of life.

Casting all on Christ. "No one of you can be My disciple who does not give up all his possessions" (Luke 14:33). God isn't calling us to communism or socialism. It was true that in the Jerusalem church people made the volitional choice to pool their possessions and give to people according to their needs. That was a choice they made. But that is not normative for the church today. God is not against the free enterprise system and he is not against people making money for the glory of God. This verse teaches us that we must not try to cling to material things. We must yield ourselves and everything we have to the Lord. Someone has said, "All that God has is available to the one who is available to all that God has."

If we are going to get all of God's fullness in our lives and experience the great joy in this life, we must give him everything. We must make a decision between two options in our lives. Either we allow Jesus Christ to work through us totally and totally yield ourselves to him or we lose what God wants us to have. We will serve God or Satan. We must choose one and then go all the way. We must be hot or cold—we must not be lukewarm in regard to his cross.

ASSIGNMENT

1. Evaluate your life in light of the seven characteristics of a progressing disciple.
2. If you are not sure Jesus Christ has entered your life, invite him in as your Savior and Lord once and for all. Simply agree with him that you are sinful and accept him into your life as the One who died for you. Do it now.
3. If you know you have Christ in your life, recommit *every area* of your life to him. Ask the Lord Jesus to control you by the power of his Holy Spirit. By faith begin to believe that the same power that raised Christ from the dead will flow through you.

SIX
KNOWING WHAT GOD WANTS US TO BE

Many of us climb the ladder of success only to find that it was leaning against the wrong wall. We work and work sincerely to achieve success but find that when we have reached what we thought was the top, we still are not successful in any sense of the term. We still feel unfulfilled and hollow.

"Against which wall, exactly, does one set his ladder?" someone may ask.

"Against God's wall for him," the answer comes.

"But how does one know which wall that is?" another may ask. Another way to state that question is "How does God reveal his will to us?"

To answer that question we see that there are three voices that God's Holy Spirit uses to communicate his will to us.

PRACTICED TRUTH
God's major tool to teach us his will is his practiced truth— God's word applied. Paul prayed: "We have not ceased to pray for you and to ask that you may be filled with the knowledge of His will in all spiritual wisdom and understanding, so that you may walk in a manner worthy of the Lord, to please Him in all respects, bearing fruit in every good work and increasing in the knowledge of God" (Col. 1:9, 10).

65

If a person wants to walk in the right way, to climb the right wall, he must know God's will, especially as revealed in his Word. Three words are used in this passage about knowing God's Word: knowledge, understanding, and wisdom.

Knowledge is the accumulation of facts. It is important to know the facts pertaining to what one is to do. But accumulation of facts alone is meaningless. For, "knowledge (alone) puffs up (makes one proud) but love (knowledge applied) edifies." Information without application equals stagnation. But information with application equals transformation. Since God wants our transformation, we must go beyond basic knowledge.

Paul stated that to knowledge we must add *understanding*, which is the ability to perceive the application of truth and apply it to life. For instance, I might know that I should love someone, but I do not show my understanding of what love is until I begin to practice it. For example, when I show patience toward someone I love, love is being practiced. By doing so, I prove my understanding. The great need to move from basic knowledge to understanding is expressed by Solomon: "Incline your hearts to understanding. . . . lift your voice for understanding" (Prov. 2:2, 3).

But even knowledge and understanding are not enough. We must "make our ears attentive to wisdom" (Prov. 2:2). *Wisdom* is the full understanding of a principle that I have after I have repeatedly applied that principle to my life. Regular obedience and meditation provides the insights known as wisdom. The Holy Spirit uniquely gives wisdom, whereas knowledge and understanding come more directly from the Scriptures. Note Solomon's statement in Proverbs 2:6: "For the Lord gives wisdom; out of His mouth [the Bible] comes knowledge and understanding."

God wants us to have this full sense of knowledge of his will, but it will come only as we gain the insights of knowledge, understanding, and wisdom. The one essential element that runs through each stage is the application of the known truth. If we apply the truth, we will "increase in the knowledge of God." If we do not apply the truth to our lives, we will only increase in the knowledge of facts. And these alone will cause stagnation and not progress. Solomon urged us to: "Cry for discernment, lift your voices for understanding; if you seek her as silver, and search for her as for hidden treasure; then you will discern the fear of the Lord, and discover the knowledge of God" (Prov. 2:3-5).

The same concept is seen in the New Testament. Jesus said: "He who has My commandments, and keeps them, he it is who loves Me; and he who loves Me shall be loved by My Father, and I will love him, and disclose Myself to him" (John 14:21). If we want God's presence, his reality, his intimate will in our lives, we must obey what we already know. If we keep progressing from knowledge of facts to the understanding of implications to the wisdom of repeated application, God's will and reality will be progressively true in our lives. That is why we must say with David, "O how I love Thy law! It is my meditation all the day" (Ps. 119:97).

The Word of God (applied), offers us the basic structure for the wall against which we place our ladder of success. However, there are other elements to that wall. One of those added elements or tools that God uses is *people*. God brings certain people into our lives through whom he sometimes speaks.

GOD USES PEOPLE
God wants us to gain insights from the tools he uses. For us to progress in our lives we must be made aware of areas that need to grow. We might indulge in overt sins of commission or sins of omission. God sometimes puts people in our lives to cause us to grow. He might use subtle lessons to keep our ears and eyes open and teachable.

One of my weaknesses, for example, is overeating—I love food, especially doughnuts. There is nothing wrong with *liking* doughnuts, but I really *love* them! On numerous occasions I have had to drive past one particular doughnut shop that even the thought of it awakens incredible delectable visions from a mile in either direction. I could almost smell their doughnuts, see them, taste them.

I know that is amusing, but for me it is also a sin. I told some of my friends about this problem and they began asking me every time they saw me if I had had a doughnut recently. Do you know how irritating that is? But, it worked. God wanted my progressive, continual victory in this area, and so he used people to help me.

A more subtle illustration is my sweet and loud daughter, Molly. I loved to hold her and kiss her, but I fell apart when she cried or screamed. Sometimes I felt like gagging her when she was screaming. But God used that person in my life to help me progress. I must not react but respond to God's tool—Molly. If I do not, God will bring in another tool—a bigger one.

The tool God uses is not always so pleasant. Sometimes, it is a sledgehammer—someone out to get us—an adversary. God has brought tools like that into my life periodically. Sometimes it is a person who talks behind my back or a person who is an outright enemy.

Recently a friend of mine, a close business associate, glared at me right in the eye and said, "I hate you with every fibre of my being and I will never forgive you." Well, I said, "I can appreciate that. There are others who feel the same way. What have I done?" I asked. So he let me have it—he told me. Now I could have reacted to this unpleasant experience by becoming defensive and tuning the fellow out completely or by becoming so crushed and introspective that I would have been totally immobile.

However, I sought to respond to God's tool. Though much of my friend's attack on me sprang from some personal problems he was having, there was some truth to what he was saying about me. I had to listen and learn. It was painful, but needed if I was to make progress in my life.

GOD USES PROBLEMS

Not only does God show me his walk of success through practical success and people, but also through certain *problems*. Robert Schuller poignantly states, "Every problem is pregnant with possibilities!" Problems will make us or break us. If we react to them, they will break us, but if we respond and learn from them, they will make us.

A most decriptive passage on this topic is found in James. "When all kinds of trials and tribulations crowd into our lives, my brethren, don't resent them as intruders, but welcome them as friends" (James 1:2, Phillips). Now doesn't that appear to be the most perverted logic ever heard? When troubles crowd into our lives (disease, tragedy, annoyances, disharmony, set backs, deaths, etc.) we are not to treat them as though they were intruding into our lives. James did not say to accept them, but to welcome them as friends—gratefully, joyously, with open arms, to embrace them. Why?

The answer is what follows. "Knowing that the testing of your faith produces endurance. And let endurance have its perfect result, that you may be perfect and complete, lacking in nothing" (James 1:3, 4). God wants us to be like Paul, who said, "I have learned to be content in whatever circumstances I am. I know how to get along with humble means, and I also know how to live in prosperity; in any and every circumstance, I have learned the secret of being filled and going hungry, both of having abundance and suffering need. I can do all things through Him who strengthens me" (Phil. 4:11-13).

Circumstances did not determine Paul's joy. Jesus did. The same is true of us. Then we will be "perfect and complete, lacking in nothing." Many good things will never fill that void. Only the attitude of joyous response to every circumstance—good and bad.

God uses problems to make us dependent upon him and therefore, "complete, wanting nothing." This truth can be visualized as a set of equations:

Problems + Rejoicing (welcoming them as friends)= Endurance
Endurance + Repetition= Completeness (wanting nothing/fulfillment)

But,

Problem + Griping= Frustration
Frustration + Repetition= Bitterness and Death.

When I have a cold, I am miserable. I want everyone to have sympathy for me. I want my wife to wait on me, hand and foot. I want people to understand that I cannot help being a griper, negative, sharp, and generally irritable. But the passage in James teaches that when I feel ill I am to rejoice. I do not have to be happy; I just have to rejoice—welcome my cold as a friend and not resent it. That produces endurance and as endurance begins to work within me, I gain greater patience and a sense of fulfillment in my relationship with Jesus alone. Circumstances are never to make or break me. Jesus is my source of fulfillment.

Practical truth, people, and problems all make up that wall against which we are to lean our ladders to success.

Solomon wrote of this kind of success. "He is on the path of life who heeds instruction. But he who forsakes reproof goes astray" (Prov. 10:17). "He whose ear listens to the life-giving reproof will dwell among the wise. He who neglects discipline despises himself, but he who listens to reproof acquires understanding" (Prov. 15:31, 32). "He who hates reproof will die" (Prov. 15:10) "A man who hardens his neck after much reproof will suddenly be broken beyond remedy" (Prov. 29:1).

ASSIGNMENT

For a practical application of these principles, a worksheet is given below:

1. List at least two specific tools God has used this past week to get your attention and to teach you.

Area	Situation	Your Response	Lessons to be Learned	Proper Response
Practiced truth 1.				
2.				
3.				
People 1.				
2.				
3.				

70

Problems   1.

             2.

             3.

2. Practice responding to one of these areas this next week.

3. Keep up your daily log and record your progress.

SEVEN
CHARACTER
DEVELOPMENT

As Christians, we say our major purpose is to glorify God. But what does glorifying God mean? If we see evangelism and discipleship as major means to glorify God, the tendency is to move toward activity as our purpose. Very subtly, we can get caught up in a whirl of doing the Lord's work. As a result, we have based our work with the Lord on *what and how much we do* and not on *who we are*.

We first glorify God through who we are. One way is to worship him. Worship is more than simply ascribing worth to God or saying to God and his creatures that God is worthy. Worship involves who we are, our life-styles, and our attitudes. Attitude is important since it lies behind all that we are and do. For instance, if a Christian is sharing his faith daily and actively involved in discipling others with a negative, grumbling attitude, these activities are not glorifying to God. Glorifying God means to return to him what he is due: worship is what we say, what we do, and who we are.

Personal worship involves experiencing the Lord, actually enjoying him. One of the pitfalls in our attempt to combat liberal theology has been to eliminate the subjective, experiential part of the Christian life. We have become so objective that we have, in many cases, lost the joy of simply practicing God's presence.

The author of Hebrews said that we have entered into a "Sabbath rest." We no longer are limited to a single day set aside for worship, although that one day is important. Our moment-by-moment life is a Sabbath. We are to practice God's presence every minute of every day. The character God wants to develop in us is a life of constant worship. Certain characteristics are present in such a life. The acrostic of the word PRESENCE may help us to remember them.

P—PRAISE GOD CONTINUALLY

We should praise God as a way of life for who he is and what he has done. The Psalmist wrote: "That the presence of God inhabits the praise of His people" (Ps. 22:3).

When people corporately and individually praise God with an attitude of expectation, God is actively present, or inhabits their praise. An example of this is found in 2 Chronicles. When Jehoshaphat was facing a hopeless situation, and his nation was surrounded and outnumbered by the armies of three tribes, the nation of Judah faced certain destruction. What were they to do? God said to Jehoshaphat, "Do not fear or be dismayed for the battle is not yours but God's" (2 Chron. 20:15). Instead of fighting the next day they stood up to praise God (v. 19). How strange it must have seemed to begin praising God while the surrounding enemy was ready to strike! We know from that historical account that the enemy armies of that day killed off their captives. It was as if the praise by God's people confused Satan. God was actively present among his praising people.

How should we respond when we face problems or difficulties? Our primary response should be to start praising God. When we praise God in difficult situations, he is free to move mightily on our behalf. When there is praise, there is the active presence of God. Where there is the presence of God, there is praise. This is true not only in individual lives, but also in the corporate life of the church. When the body begins to praise God corporately, he starts to move in a mighty way. God delights in the praise and starts to move. There are three important parts to praising God.

1. Praise God *continually.* In Psalm 34:1 we read: "I will bless the Lord at all times; His praise shall continually be in my mouth." That means we should praise God when we get up in the morning—for some of us that takes real faith—until we go to bed early at night. If I don't begin my day praising God, I find many times I go through the day with a negative spirit. But if I can turn my praise back to God, my attitude changes. That concept of turning my praise to God relates to the second point.

2. Praise God *volitionally,* as an act of the will. Psalm 57:7 talks about David choosing to praise God. He wrote: "I will bless the Lord." He did not say, "I feel like blessing the Lord." He said, "I *will* bless the Lord." He made a habit out of it.

3. Praise God *melodically.* In Psalm 150:3-6, musical praise is encouraged. In Ephesians 5:19 we find if we are filled with the Spirit we will "speak to one another in psalms and hymns and spiritual songs, rejoicing and making melody in our hearts to the Lord." There is a natural outflow. Paul wrote: "teaching and admonishing one another with psalms and hymns and spiritual songs, singing with thankfulness in your hearts to God" (Col. 3:16), the response of a heart in which the Word of God dwells richly. Praise is a natural outflow of our intimate relations with the Lord.

R—REJOICE IN NEGATIVE CIRCUMSTANCES

We are told to rejoice or give thanks over one hundred times in the New Testament alone. "In everything give thanks; for this is the will of God for you in Christ Jesus" (1 Thess. 5:18). Thanksgiving is simply what I call "the attitude of gratitude." Our lives are to be permeated with an attitude of sweetness and graciousness toward God and toward others. Paul wrote: "Do all things without grumbling or disputing" (Phil. 2:14).

E—EXPERIENCE THE LORD IN LOW POINTS

Psalm 38 is a prayer of David after committing adultery with Bathsheba and murdering her husband as well. He was experiencing a low point in his life because of sin. The first verses are his response to his guilt:

75

O, Lord, rebuke me not in Thy wrath, and chasten me not in Thy burning anger. For Thine arrows have sunk deep into me, and Thy hand has pressed down on me. There is no soundness in my flesh because of Thine indignation; there is no health in my bones because of my sin. For my iniquities are gone over my head; as a heavy burden they weigh too much for me. My wounds grow foul and fester. Because of my folly, I am bent over and greatly bowed down; I go mourning all day long. For my loins are filled with burning; and there is no soundness in my flesh. I am benumbed and badly crushed; I groan because of the agitation of my heart. Lord, all my desire is before Thee; and my sighing is not hidden from Thee. [Psalm 38:1-9]

We get the feeling that David was hurting at this point. Some of us have hurt like that. All of us are going to have low points in our lives.

I attended a meeting one night several years ago. It was an organizational meeting for a ministry with which I was involved. During that meeting with some of my good friends, I was raked over the coals. Now usually I have a pretty good self-concept, and can handle criticism. But this particular night I felt betrayed by a friend. I had never been so emotionally low in my life. I drove home and sat in front of my house in the car. It was 2:00 A.M., and I was emotionally, physically, and spiritually drained. I could not pray and I did not want to read the Bible. Normally, when we are down, the last thing we want to do is turn to the Lord. And yet, that is the time when God wants to use these circumstances to teach us something about our lives.

David experienced some great truths in his life because when he was down he was open before the Lord. As I sat in my car, I began to cry uncontrollably. I was on the verge of anger, bitterness, and frustration over the events of the night. That is when God allowed me to sing the only song I could think of at that time:

Jesus loves me, this I know,
For the Bible tells me so.
Little ones to him belong;
They are weak but he is strong.
Yes, Jesus loves me, Yes, Jesus loves me,
Yes, Jesus loves me.
The Bible tells me so.

As I sang that song over and over, God did a miracle in my life. He changed my attitude completely. I was grieved for a while, but not bitter. I was hurt, but not angry. God gave me a new perspective by reminding me that I was here to please him—not people. He was causing all things to work together for good. The most important thing I needed to know was that he loved me. He was going to care for me in the days that followed.

I started to keep a log of all that God was doing in my life. I got more profound insights than ever before, because God was able to meet me at a point of great personal inadequacy. He began showing me that it is all right to have times when we are emotionally up and times when we are emotionally down. High and low points are not marks of spirituality but a mark of physiology. We must turn to God in our low points. It may also be helpful to keep a log or a diary as we experience highs and lows in our lives. We should ask God to give us special insights into him and his Word as we experience him in our low points.

S— SEEK THE LORD

"But seek first His kingdom and His righteousness; and all these things shall be added to you" (Matt. 6:33). "But from there you will seek the Lord your God, and you will find Him if you search for Him with all your heart and all your soul" (Deut. 4:29). "Seek the Lord and His strength; seek His face continually" (1 Chron. 16:11). "The Lord has looked down from heaven upon the sons of men, to see if there are any who understand, who seek after God" (Ps. 14:2).

Over and over in Scripture we are told to seek the Lord. That

77

is difficult because everything in life today is geared toward being a spectator. We are used to letting other people do the work while we receive the benefits. The tendency is for us to sit back and take, instead of going forward after God with all our hearts and minds. I believe God is looking for men and women who are aggressively seeking him.

Seeking the Lord is trying to find him and meet him where he is. One way that we seek the Lord is through meditation, as we discussed earlier.

E—EXPECT THE MIRACULOUS

A girl once said to me, "Ron, you have the gift of faith." I am not really sure I have the gift of faith or not, but the girl's statement encouraged me to the point of believing God for miracles.

It was at that point that I realized that it was not my *great* faith in God that counted, but it was my faith in a *great God* that was the basis for miracles. Faith is not something we have to conjure up. God will give us all the faith we need as we learn to trust him and build his Word into our lives.

I need to believe God for the miraculous in two areas, for my character and the character of others. Christians need to learn to believe God for radical character transformation in the lives of people. We need to pray very specifically that God will root out blind spots and sin problems in our lives and the lives of other believers. I also need to expect the miraculous in my personal ministry.

N—NEED GOD

How much do we need God? People have probably asked us this before, but we need to think about it again.

If the Holy Spirit had not been resident within us this last week, how would our lives have been different? Could we have acted the same way we acted, had the same thoughts we had without the Holy Spirit being there?

There are probably varying degrees of it, but how much do we need God? What demonstration is there in our lives that we need God? I think we need to learn to need God. We need to learn to sing the song, "I need Thee every hour."

If we read the histories of great men and women of God, we will find that they were men and women who had an abject dependence upon God. They said, "If God doesn't do it, it can't be done."

That affects the way we live and the manner in which we turn to him. How much do we pray about little things? The problem is that we can do a lot without God, can't we? We have learned to maneuver pretty well, but God says there are things that he wants us to do that we can do only as we have a sense of need for him. As the sense of need grows, he will open up things for us that we can believe him for.

C—CONFESS REGULARLY
"We know all about confession because we have learned to walk in the Spirit" someone might say. The Spirit-filled life has been popularized today, so it can become a rote habit like anything else.

"Spiritual breathing" (exhaling the bad by confessing our sins and inhaling the good by putting the Spirit in control again) is so easy that we can become insensitive to the significance it should play in our lives. The only good thing about sin is that it turns us back to God. Confession should not consist merely of recognizing the sin, but also of admitting to God that we have hurt him, thanking him for his unconditional love and forgiveness, repenting or turning away from that sin and accepting his forgiveness. Whenever we sin we must simply confess our sin and accept his forgiveness. We must not allow Satan to discourage us and inhibit God's power in our lives.

E—ENJOY THE LORD
"O taste and see that the Lord is good" (Ps. 34:8). That is the same concept as in Psalm 37:4, "Delight thyself in the Lord." Implications of delighting in and enjoying God carry over into personal relationships, too. We need to learn to enjoy people. Everybody is unique—believers and unbelievers alike. We

can enjoy God by enjoying people, revelling in our uniqueness and similarities. The same is true of nature. The nature of God was made for God's glory, that we would glorify him and enjoy him forever. We are not here to live for ourselves, but if we respond to God we will have great joy in our lives.

ASSIGNMENT
1. Memorize the PRESENCE acrostic
2. Use the acrostic as you meditate four times a day for about forty days in a row.

EIGHT
DEVELOPING UNITY
IN THE BODY

"I love the world; it's just people I can't stand." This comment, by Charlie Brown of *Peanuts* cartoon fame, typifies the attitude of many Christians today. Yet no one, Christian or non-Christian, can really claim to be successful without demonstrating love toward other people.

As Christians we are responsible for forging good relationships with others. "Let us consider how to stimulate one another to love and good deeds, not forsaking our own assembling together, as is the habit of some, but encouraging one another; and all the more, as you see the day drawing near" (Heb. 10:24, 25). The author of Hebrews was not talking about sitting back and receiving right relationships—he was suggesting that we take the initiative in developing them. So the first responsibility in successful relationships is to take the initiative.

Another important responsibility is given by Paul in writing to the Philippians: "Do nothing from selfish or empty conceit, but with humility of mind, let each of you regard another as more important than himself" (Phil. 2:3). Putting others before ourselves is how we live as successful Christians. To develop this kind of love for others is to develop unity within the body of Christ. In John 17, the Lord's great prayer was for unity: "I do not ask on behalf of the world but for those whom Thou hast given Me.... that they may all be one.... perfected in unity, that the world may know Thou hast sent Me" (John 17:9, 21, 23).

Because Satan knows the power of unity, he seeks to destroy it. That is why we are sometimes filled with all sorts of hateful thoughts about other people. For instance, we may walk into a room, someone looks at us, and we think, "He hates me. I saw the way he looked at me. He hates me." You may say, "Nobody is that paranoid!" When Satan begins to plant ideas in people's heads, their reactions can be just that unfounded, even if not that extreme.

There are several specific things we can do to develop unity within the body. We can uplift one another, we can accept our need for one another, we can develop the right kind of intimate relations with others, we can develop trust for one another, and we can yield to one another—each of these having sound biblical basis.

UPLIFTING ONE ANOTHER

This concept comes from the biblical word "encouragement" or "exhortation." It is used many, many times in the New Testament. Exhortation comes from two Greek terms: *para,* meaning "along side" and *kaleo,* meaning "to call." It is the word from which we get "paraclete." We exhort people when we call them along side to encourage them or to reprove them. Some have suggested that it could be used of a general standing before his troops. They have just lost the battle and he wants them to win the war. So he tries to encourage them so they are emotionally and mentally uplifted so that they will choose to go out and win the war.

We are to encourage people, to call them alongside, to lift them up, to motivate them. We can do that by complimenting, expressing confidence in them, and comforting them.

Compliments are different from flattery. Flattery usually involves praise for things over which a person has no control while compliments recognize character growth or things a person is doing or producing. Where it is probably not a good idea to say, "You are smart," it is good to say, "I appreciate the way you study so hard."

James Dobson, well-known psychologist and writer, advises parents that children not be praised or criticized for looks or intellect, things over which they have no control. This flattery or criticism begins to be the measuring rod for self-worth, creating self-concepts based on the world's view of success and not God's view. The Lord complimented character qualities. A study of his approach to people shows how much he encouraged people and praised them for their character and things God was building into their lives.

We should never degrade people. We should stay away from flippant statements, sarcasm, and cynicism. Instead we should try to build up people with what we say.

When I played peewee football, we had an A-team, a B-team, a C-team, and a D-team. On the D-team we had first and second string—I played on second string—the very worst. During my "heavy" days, I was known as Jelly Belly Jenson. I was not known for my lightning speed. I was so heavy I could play center, guard, and tackle all at the same time. My dream, true of any lineman, was to get a fumbled football, pick it up, and run for a touchdown. I was playing defense one day, and somehow the other team fumbled. I picked up the ball and started running with it. I realized I was going the wrong way when I heard cheers from the wrong side of the field and when one of my teammates tackled me. My teammates rubbed that in for years. "Wrong way Jenson," they started calling me. It had an indelible effect upon my life because I was thought of as stupid, which contributed to the low self-concept I struggled with as a boy.

Every day we should say something encouraging to somebody, to lift them up, to compliment them. People are not usually motivated by hearing what they are doing wrong, but by hearing what they are doing right. Sometimes we need to admonish people but much more often we need to be positive in what we say to them.

We uplift one another by expressing our *confidence* in each other. In the upper room, there were twelve men, most of whom had fallen away from following Christ. Some had been with him for three years; they had seen him and his miracles, the verification of his deity. They had heard that he was going to die and rise again, but when he was crucified, they thought that was it. Then they were together with Jesus in the upper room. If it had been me, I probably would have said to them, "You traitors. I spent three years pouring myself into you, labored hard; I go to pray and you fall asleep. I tell you what to do and you don't do it. I teach you and train you. I could have ministered to all those people, but, no, I didn't do that—I spent all my time with you, and then you fail me."

But the Lord did not say that at all. He told them that if they didn't get the job done it wouldn't be done. He entrusted everything to them. Jesus motivated them not by hitting them when they were down but by lifting them up.

Howard Hendricks, a popular writer and teacher, tells a story about his grade school days. He said he was so rowdy that his fifth grade teacher had to tie his hands and feet to keep him in his chair, and sometimes even gag him. His reputation went before him into sixth grade. He recalled vividly going into his sixth grade class the first day and seeing a teacher whom he said appeared about seven feet tall. She looked down at him and said, "So you are Howie Hendricks. I have heard a lot about you." And then she knelt down and looked at him right in the eyes and said, "and I do not believe a word of it." He said he was an angel all year long because someone believed in him.

People are being put down so much that they often need someone to believe in them to speak, as it were, good things into reality.

I remember a girl who sang with me in a Youth for Christ choir. I was striving for God's best for my life and one day she said to me, "Ron, you have the gift of faith."

I asked "How do you know?"

She said, "I have the gift of discernment." I believed her. I started believing God for great miracles—things I had never asked for before. I started to believe that I had the gift of faith.

I don't really think I did, but because someone visualized achievement, I started to believe that I could do it. We never achieve until we believe we can. We need to have people all the time saying, "I believe you and I think God is going to do great things through you."

We also uplift others by *comforting* them. Paul wrote that we should comfort others with the same comfort wherewith we have been comforted (2 Cor. 1:3-5). We need to get along side of people who hurt, empathize with them, and love them just the way they arc. Comforting is a great evangelistic tool. If we build relationships with people in our neighborhoods, God may eventually open an opportunity to comfort them. When they see the reality of Christ in our lives and how God has taken us through hard times that might be somewhat similar to their problems, we may have some credibility.

The first thing we need to do in building unity is to uplift one another daily.

NEEDING ONE ANOTHER
The body of Christ needs us and we need the body of Christ. Part of building unity is demonstrated by our activities involving other people. That is very hard for some people—it is hard for me. I find it easy to speak to large groups but find it hard to work on a one-to-one basis. When people start ministering to me one-to-one, I have problems. I find that I am so activity oriented, and tend to have a "giving out" mentality, I have a hard time letting others minister to me. Yet, I know I need it. Whether or not you feel you need others, you do. You need to be *stimulated* by others to grow. God did not make us to live the Christian life alone.

INTIMATELY RELATING TO ONE ANOTHER
Building unity means intimately relating to others, which involves both *communicating* and correcting. An old English word for intimate communication is "intercourse." It has come to mean only the physical coming together of two people, but the original word "intimacy" really describes much more than

85

physical closeness as we have generally understood it to be. It is the deepest level of communication, the kind we normally experience with a spouse. We may develop the ability to share with one, two, or three other people with whom we have very deep commitments. All of us need to develop deeper levels of communication with at least one other person.

There are at least five levels of communication, someone has said. The first is the cliché level, which sounds something like this: "Hi, how are you?" "Fine, good to see you," sentiments neither speaker necessarily felt. Sometimes people use such meaningless clichés as part of their prayers to God.

A second level of communication is the exchange of facts. Such communication does not reveal much about the person talking. When asked for an opinion, someone communicating at this level will instead offer another person's opinions rather than risking relection of his own.

The third level is sharing one's own opinions with another. We have all perhaps been in meetings where we are talking about an issue and someone says, "Now all of you who agree, raise your hands." People rather sheepishly sneak up a hand, often looking around first to see what others are doing. The reason they hesitate is that they do not want to be branded as being different. There is such a pressure to be alike that sometimes we don't like to share our own opinions. Sharing opinions makes for a very fertile ground for growth. When I share my opinion, I am getting sown into the depth of issues.

People often try to build unity in churches by getting everyone to think the same way. That does not necessarily build unity. In fact, probably many of them do not agree—they just act as though they do. Disagreement can be healthy. I have been in good church meetings where disagreements are not personal affronts but expressions of different, and often helpful, perspectives. Some things were never resolved in our meetings but the meetings were anything but unspiritual. There was still a spirit of unity though opinions differed.

The fourth level of communication is the sharing or expression of feelings. Very early in our marriage, my wife offered to do my filing of correspondence and study notes. I love to have things filed, to have everything in the right box, in the right space, at the right time. If not, I feel insecure. A couple of days went by and she had not filed. I said, "Honey, you have not filed."

She said, "Oh, I'll do it by Friday." Friday came and she had not filed.

I said, "Honey, you said you were going to file."

She answered, "Right, I will have it done by the weekend."

The weekend was over and I said, "Honey, you have not had a chance to file yet, have you?"

She responded, "Oh, I keep forgetting about it." And there is where it started to happen. I began to think, "She doesn't love me; in fact, she doesn't even like me. In fact, she is probably trying to torture me. She knows, anybody would know how important it is to file." So finally I sat down with her and I said, "Honey, let me tell you what I feel like when you do not file. I feel insecure. All day long I go around wondering where those papers are if I need to get at them." When she realized how strongly I felt about her filing, her attitude and motivation changed. People can't respond to our feelings if they don't know how we feel.

Two labels can not be affixed to feelings. We cannot label a feeling as stupid because we cannot interpret other people's feelings in light of our own. And we cannot term other's feelings invalid. We need to learn how to understand how and why other people respond the way they do.

Understanding at the "feelings" level of communication requires that we learn how to get feedback from one another. When we are intimately relating to people we are trying to get back intimate feedback so we are continually seeking responses.

Recently I heard about a man whose wife had just read *Total Woman*. When he came home one night, she was all ready for him—candlelight dinner, the children out for the evening, a special dinner, and she was appropriately attired. He came in the door. She was waiting there for him—the lights were low.

He looked at her and said, "Hi, what's for dinner?" He then walked to the table, sat down without comment, ate half his favorite meal and then walked out, hardly talking to her at all.

Two nights later, he and his wife went to his mother's house for a macaroni and cheese dinner. He hated macaroni and cheese and yet he said, "It's the best meal I've had in months." His wife was sitting there thinking, "He hates me." As they were driving home he said, "Wasn't that a nice evening?"

She answered, "You have got the gall to call that a nice evening? I have had it with you right up to my neck. I do everything I can to serve you. I feed you a good meal and prepare for a nice evening at home, and you don't even care—you don't even notice. You do not love me any more. I want a divorce."

He sat back and asked "I just said, 'Wasn't that a nice evening' and you want a divorce?"

She did not know that the reason he praised his mother was because he was convinced his mother had a very poor self-concept. He felt guilty that he had not appreciated his mother while growing up. He used to laugh at her macaroni and cheese. And he bent over backwards to praise her because he felt guilty about his past indifference and wanted to demonstrate his love to his mother. But he didn't realize that the way he was going about building up his mother's self-image was destroying his wife's.

Neither did his wife know that the reason he rushed in and rushed out the night of her special efforts was because his boss had put him under tremendous pressure. He came home because he wanted to have dinner with his wife, but he had to go right back to another dinner that his boss insisted upon and that had a great deal to do with his job. It had nothing to do with his feelings for her.

Who was wrong—the wife or the husband? He was wrong in not communicating to his wife. And she was wrong in not communicating with him.

The final level of communication is complete openness. Complete intimacy involves complete honesty and transparency. The more transparent we can be, which only comes from a secure self-image, the more effective our ministry will be. People respond to transparency because it is not threatening to them.

We intimately relate to one another by *correcting* other people in the right way. Admonition should be positive. It is part of biblical love, and it is part of unity. Sin can't be allowed to remain in camp too long or it develops a tremendous break in the unity of the body. We need to learn how to deal with it in a positive and healthy way.

On the trip we made with another couple we were discussing the need to be flexible in general and specifically in regards to our travel schedule. I said, "Amen, we do need to be flexible."

After a while, my companions said to me, "Ron, you are not very flexible."

"Me? not flexible? Of course, I am flexible!"

But they cared enough to admonish me in this area because they knew I needed it.

One day I was at a Seafair Parade in Seattle, Washington. I had just come back from Arrowhead Springs and had been trained in a method of one-to-one evangelism. I saw a nice looking man walking up and down the road in front of people. He had a satchel at his side. He wasn't talking to anyone—just passing out tracts. I built up what I thought was righteous indignation. I thought, "He has got the gall to cram tracts in the faces of people and not talk to them!" Some would read his leaflets and smile, some would laugh at him, and others would throw them down. I thought, "What an awful testimony he is for Christ! He should be talking to the people, explaining the gospel to them." Finally I walked up to him.

I grabbed him by his shoulder and turned him around. "Excuse me," I said, "You are a Christian, and I am too. Why do you just cram tracts into peoples' faces? Why don't you talk to them?"

He tried to answer, "... aaaaaaa..." He could not talk! He had a speech impediment. As I tried to melt into the cement, my future flashed before me. I saw a big line in heaven with the "biggies" up front and the little people in the back of the line. I saw him right up in the front and I saw myself very near the back.

I thought, "I can talk, I can speak to people; and I'm not even doing that! This guy is using all that he has and I'm trying to tell him what he ought to do!" I was ashamed. Needless to say, that is not the way to admonish.

From Matthew 18:15-20 and Galatians 6:1, we can extract several principles to follow in admonishing others.

1. Admonish *prayerfully*. Pray that God will change the person without your having to talk to him. Talking to someone is always the last resort. If God does not change them, and if he wants us to be part of the instrument, then we must pray that God will make them responsive to what we have to share.

2. Admonish *personally and privately*. Never admonish in a crowd. One exception to that might be the occasion when elders are caught in a sin. Paul wrote to Timothy that they should not consider an offense against an elder unless it is observed by two or more witnesses and then, if he is found guilty, and continues in his sin, the elder is to be rebuked in the presence of the whole church in order that the people might fear (1 Tim. 5:19, 20). But it appears from the context that before the public rebuke he should be warned privately to give him an opportunity to turn from his sin. If he persists, then of course the church has no choice but to give the public rebuke.

3. Admonish *passionately*, with a full heart. We do not admonish flippantly if we really care about people.

4. Admonish *positively*, stating strengths as well as weaknesses.

5. Admonish *practically*. Offer constructive, practical help. Someone once told me that he didn't like me. I asked what it was he didn't like and he said, "Your personality." I said, "Could you be a bit more specific?"

"No," he said, "it's all of you I don't like."

I am aware that there are many things about myself that I ought to try to change. But that kind of admonition did no good at all.

90

6. Admonish *progressively*. Matthew 18 speaks of a progression to follow in admonishing a person when sin affects the whole church unity. One person should go, and if there is no result one or two others should be brought along, and if that is refused it should be taken to the whole assembly.

Many people are caught in terrible sins because they weren't admonished. A pastor told of an incident involving adultery of a church leader and a woman member. He knew that they were together one day, so he picked up the phone and called her. "Mary, can I talk to Bill?" (not their real names, of course).

"Bill who?" she asked.

"Mary, I know he's there, and I know what you have been doing. I would like to talk to Bill."

Bill came to the phone. His pastor said, "I know where you are, I know what you have been doing. I am here with all the elders and I tell you, dear brother, if you do not repent to God, to Mary, and to your wife, and if you do not get out of there and stay out of there, I am coming over to get you."

The man repented to everyone concerned, he got out of the woman's house and stayed out. So often we play around with sin, thinking we can avoid detection. Often God allows it to be discovered by the people who could admonish us.

A youth pastor in a church was having trouble with some of his young people. A few were smoking and selling marijuana and influencing others in the group. The youth pastor confronted the offenders and told them not to come back if they were going to continue with the marijuana. They laughed at him. So the whole process of church discipline began.

Finally the pastor said to these boys, "If you do not stop your involvement with marijuana, you cannot come back here. If I catch you in church I will physically take you out.

These boys needed to test the limits, so the next Sunday they walked into church. The pastor got out from behind the pulpit, walked down the aisle, walked into the pew, grabbed them by the arms, and in front of everybody, marched them outside the church. No one had ever followed through with these boys. Their parents had shown them their fences, but instead of holding them inside them and making them pay the consequences, the parents simply made the fences broader.

Several years later one of those young men became youth pastor of that church because somebody caught him and held him accountable. That is an example of what admonition can do. God forbid that we admonish people because they are different from us. But God forbid that we don't admonish people when we see sin in their lives and do not have enough love for them to try to help them.

TRUSTING ONE ANOTHER

Love thinks the best of others. Love doesn't think negatively about situations. I remember I was asked once to bring extra chairs for a dinner I was attending. It was held at the home of one of our elders, one that I respected the most. When I got there he asked me about the chairs. "I forgot," I said. He looked at me and said, "That figures."

I started thinking, what does he mean, "That figures"? He thinks I am incompetent. He thinks I always forget things. And God said to me, "Ron you have got two choices; either you think the best about what he said, assume it did not mean anything negative towards you and forget it. Or, you can go talk to him and ask him what he meant."

Out of cowardice I said, "I'll forget it." Two weeks later I saw him in the hall at the church and decided I would ask him about it. So I went up to him and said, "You know the other night when I forgot to bring the chairs? You said, 'That figures.' "

"Oh, I shouldn't have said that," he said.

"That's what I thought." I went on to say, "But you did say that and I'm curious just why and what you meant."

He said, "Well, I had seven meetings that day and all day long people had forgotten important things needed for the meeting."

See what I was doing? I thought he was referring to me. He was referring rather to the kind of day it had been for him.

YIELDING TO ONE ANOTHER

We yield ourselves to one another in humbleness and humility of mind, by esteeming others better than ourselves.

Unity within the body is a mark of personal success as well as corporate success. We cannot say truthfully that we are successful individuals if we are not contributing significantly to the corporate success of the body of Christ to which we are personally associated. We should learn to improve on Charlie Brown's statement. We should be able to say, "I love the world—I know I do, because I love people."

ASSIGNMENT

1. Evaluate your life in light of these qualities of unity.
2. Concentrate on correcting your weakest quality this week. Do something positive each day.
3. Build these qualities into your home first.

NINE
SUCCESS—HAVING AN
IMPACT ON THE WORLD

DeTocqueville, the great French politician and statesman, was profoundly influenced by what he saw a number of years ago when he studied in the United States. Upon returning home to his native France he said, "America is great because it is good, but if America ever ceases to be good, it will cease to be great."

Today, as never before, America is beginning to lose its goodness. We are experiencing problems unparalleled in our history. Never have we been more without direction. Never have we been in a bleaker situation. Even in the founding days of this country, when the nation was facing a revolution, when we were facing infiltration from enemies abroad, we were not in as much danger because never before has the morale and moral fiber of American people been so low.

In his book, *Building the City of Man*, Warren Wagar sees twentieth century man as a baby in a wicker basket wailing on the doorstep of doomsday (San Francisco: W. H. Freeman, 1971).

Arnold Toynbee, a great historian, has given predictions of an emerging world government which he condeded will have to be dictatorial. The outlook for modern man in the humanistic society which he has created is bleak, he says.

Arthur Kussler has stated, "Nature has let us down. God seems to have left the receiver off the hook; the time is running out." I think the despair of American people today is superficially covered up by all sorts of outward manifestations. It is seen and typified in a letter that was written to the columnist, Ann Landers:

Dear Ann Landers,

I don't care what you do with this letter. You don't even have to read it if you don't want to but I have to write it. A lot of people wonder why anyone would want to commit suicide. Most of us have a decent life and so it seems like a crazy thing to do. But it doesn't seem so crazy to me. I'm a guy who wishes he didn't have to get up every morning and face the day. I'm 17 years old and a junior in high school. I'm empty, useless and tired of struggling. I feel like I'm in everybody's way and I don't think anybody would give a damn if I disappeared from the face of the earth. I have no idea why I was ever born. I don't fit in any place. I know you can't do anything about all this but I wanted to explain to somebody what goes through a person's mind before he pulls the trigger or swallows one too many pills. Signed, A non-person

I believe our society today has many such "non-persons." People have no direction. We have thrown out the past. We've said history has no meaning to it. We throw out the future or are afraid to face it because much of what we see in our culture moving toward the future is pessimistic, not optimistic. Things seem to be going downhill, not uphill.

INSTITUTIONAL DEMISE

The four basic institutions in society are on a very rapid downward drift. Those major institutions of family, education, government, and religion, each of which have such important ramifications on our future, are feeling the effects of our changing world.

The Family. As an institution, the family in America is falling apart. We see its deterioration in a number of ways. We see the degeneration of marriage in general. Men and women who were married in the middle 1800s had generally lived in the same geographical area. They came from the same background and when they were married they had many things in common. They came out of the same moral and philosophical background so there tended to be more harmonious marriages. But today, marriages are falling apart with tremendous rapidity. It is said that 38 percent of all first marriages fail today, and that number is increasing rapidly. Seventy-nine percent of those will remarry and 44 percent of those will divorce again. Tragically, even Christian marriages are ending in divorce in unprecedented numbers.

One of the major reasons for this increase in divorce is that the commitment to the institution of marriage has been undergoing change. Men and women believe that divorce is a viable option. Couples today say, "Instead of getting married, we'll live together and find out if we're compatible." Living together isn't marriage. The thought of a lifetime commitment being made at the altar is a rare concept today.

Many marriages have lost the sense of oneness. Even Christian marriages are often deficient. Even though Christian marriages don't end in divorce at the same frequency as non-Christian unions, many such marriages experience what some call emotional divorce. Disgruntled couples don't get a physical separation but an emotional divorce develops. A man and woman have a romantic experience, they make a commitment to one another, and then the husband seems to go one way and the wife goes another. They continue to live together but as married single people, each pursuing his own interests. There is no longer any warmth, unity, or oneness—nothing of what God intended marriage to be.

The problem often begins when Christians and non-Christians begin to date. I believe there is adequate scriptural warning against light having fellowship with darkness. We may have friends who are non-Christians. We are to love non-Christians.

We are to have commitments and positive human relationships with non-Christians, but I don't believe Christians and non-Christians should date because they are implying by dating that there is a possibility for a long-term commitment and marriage.

When couples start to go together emotions start to get involved. Often the Christian man or woman says, "That's okay, God will turn this person around; they'll come to Christ because my commitment is so great," and soon they are getting married. The Christian can't live the life that God intended he should live because he is hampered by the non-Christian. As a result there is guilt and frustration. Two different philosophies are at play. The non-Christian is frustrated and defeated; he's not attracted to Christ. He is distracted from Christ because he feels as if he is being pushed into a relationship with him. It isn't fair to the non-Christian and it isn't fair to the Christian. God doesn't want that kind of fellowship—it doesn't work.

Another reason marriages are falling apart is because of premarital and extramarital sex. God's intent has always been that sex take place in the context of a permanent relationship between one man and one woman. God loves the marriage relationship and prescribed the conditions. When a person has sexual relations before marriage he is subject to guilt feelings in marriage, the psychological implications of which are staggering. I have spent hours, in many cases hundreds of hours in marital counseling with people who are trying to handle the guilt from their own premarital and extramarital affairs. God hates premarital and extramarital sex, and it is bound to hurt those who engage in it. God intended for marriage to involve lifelong commitment. Christians should start demonstrating biblical marriage relationships and dating practices.

Thirty percent of all American couples experience some form of domestic violence in their lifetime. Two million couples have used a gun, knife, or other lethal weapon on each other during their marriage. Twenty percent of all police officers killed in the line of duty are killed while answering calls involving family conflicts. And it is estimated that between six to fifteen million women are battered in the United States each year. An interesting statistic has emerged showing that there is a growing number of battered husbands today. One of the reasons is that the leader in many homes today is no longer the man but the woman. Because of the encouragement offered by the women's lib movement, women are taking control in many homes.

One half of all the American children will spend most of their lives living with a single parent. Forty percent of adults over twenty-five are single and that number is increasing. Because of the rapid divorce rate, children are living in single parent homes, often with their mothers. God intended that a child develop under the influence and guidance of a man and a woman. Because these children aren't influenced by both mother and father roles, they are caught up in the bitterness, frustration, and defeat of divorce. They in turn develop bitterness, depression, and twisted personalities and become themselves poor candidates for healthy marriages, just as their parents were.

It is estimated that more than 200,000 American boys and girls, most below the age of five, died last year as a result of abuse by adults. It is estimated that the average time a father spends with his child per day in America is 37.6 seconds! Yet, Scripture says that the father has the primary responsibility to bring up the child in the nurture and admonition of the Lord.

All of these statistics can be summed up with one statement. "All that the family provided are now sought outside the family; sexual gratification, companionship, friendship, economic support, even procreation. The family served its purpose once, but today it is a very disruptive, destructive system." The temptation today is for the government to become more involved in the family. The government knows what the statistics are. The responsibility of the husband and wife decreases more and more because their children can be taken care of by government paid childcare situations. As a result, the responsibility is shifted more and more to the government. The family loses its effect bit by bit, even though it honestly attempts to deal with the problems. We are not going to see governmental control changed until we see a dramatic change in the family.

It is estimated that up to 50 percent of all conceptions end in abortion today. The government pays for a vast majority of those. Biblically it is hard to see any alternative but to call abortion a form of murder.

Education. Charles Malik, an educator holding over fifty honorary doctorates, was one of the founders of the United Nations and has held every major position in that organization. He says the major problem in America today is atheistic humanism in our universities. He has commented that if he could do anything today, he would develop a Christian university because he believes that our secular universities have totally embraced atheistic humanism.

Whatever begins in the mind as a result of this philosophy starts to have a negative impact. As a result, education is on a downhill trend today like never before. Three forces have devastated our educational system. One such force is *violence*. Today, violence in the classroom is unparalleled. According to the *American School Board Journal* in 1972, it was reported that teaching school was twice as dangerous as working in a steel mill. It is estimated that each year 75,000 teachers are injured badly enough to require medical attention.

According to a Senate subcommittee on juvenile delinquency, between 1964 and 1968 assaults on teachers increased by 7100 percent and unfortunately they are increasing at faster rates today. Recently, a judge in the inner city of Chicago and another judge in the inner city of Los Angeles began granting teachers hazardous duty pay for teaching in the inner city. Hazardous duty only applied before to people who worked on dangerous jobs such as loading ammunition. Our inner cities are falling apart in the area of education.

Our educational system is becoming *valueless*. Most of us have grown up in an educational system that was not based on values at all. When this country began, most of education was based on very clear moral absolutes. But today, "absolute" is a bad word. Everything is considered relative and anyone holding onto the concept of moral absolutes is considered narrow. Because everything is seen as relative, we don't communicate in an absolute value mode. As a result, people are still being influenced by values, but the values are those of their teachers and come through whatever values that teacher happens to have. More often than not, their values tend to be based on immorality and humanism rather than biblical truths, which develops an attitude within students that leads them to an unbiblical world view.

The *media* and not the classroom are the primary teaching tool of our society. It was estimated in 1976 that 336 new magazines were started in America. Most of them were geared to the teen generation and most were filled with a permissive humanistic world view that was immoral more often than not. The average time the television is on in the home in America today is 6.8 hours. Television has had a tremendous influence on us. It has dulled our senses and developed all sorts of desires within us that we are not even aware of. It has also developed a world view in us that is contrary to Scripture. From one's world view decisions are made.

Government. There is a joke out that has been used a number of times by politicians about themselves. Three men were on a long walk, a doctor, an architect, and a politician.

The doctor said, "Of course, medicine was the first profession. Remember when God created Eve? He performed surgery and took a rib out of Adam's side and fashioned Eve."

The architect said, "No, remember that God formed the world out of chaos. It was architecture."

The politician said, "But who do you think created the chaos?" How sadly that typifies government today!

I believe in America and realize that God has given us some things that we should try to maintain. I wouldn't want to be president for any amount of money. A look at the government's position today shows how tough it would be to be a leader, judging from the difficult decisions they are responsible to make these days.

Three problems plague government today. One is the burgeoning *bureaucracy*. Another problem is widespread *corruption*. You can't pick up a newspaper without reading about someone involved in scandal. Leaders are caught committing sins because they are pragmatic. Having no morality, leaders will do anything because they want to get ahead, either in power or money. The third problem is a *lack of confidence* in people.

The expensive package of bureaucracy in the United States comes lavishly wrapped in red tape. It costs business and industry and ultimately the consumer almost $20 billion a year to handle the paper work involved with government regulations. It costs government and thus the consumer another $20 billion a year to pay its printers, processors, and paper shufflers. That is $40 billion a year for triplicate forms, filing cabinets, postage stamps, and waste paper baskets. Much of it is counterproductive. It took 1,100 different permits and approvals before the construction of the Alaskan pipeline could begin. *U. S. News and World Report* recently reported that wrathful constituents were bombarding congressmen with protests against such federally funded projects as: $375,000 for a Pentagon study on the frisbee; $259,000 to teach mothers how to play with their babies; $80,000 to develop a zero gravity toilet, $121,000 to find out why some people say "ain't" and $29,000 for a study on the mating calls of the Central American toad. Money was spent this way last year in America! $600,000 in subsidy payments went to a single bee keeper in Washington, D.C. Billions are wasted annually on 900,000 totally ineligible welfare recipients, $85,000 per minute wasted to pay interest on the national debt, costing a total of $318 billion since World War II, $250 billion given in foreign aid including the financing of both sides of fourteen wars over the last twenty years.

Government is a mess! Americans do not believe in government today. *USA Today* recently reported that, "Most Americans today instinctively distrust and disbelieve their leaders." It went on to say that in the 1960s, 70 percent of Americans had a favorable view of their government. They generally trusted elected officials, and expected them to tell the truth. By the mid 1970s the figure was only 30 percent according to the social science survey. As a result of that, people don't vote and don't want to get involved because they don't think there is any viable solution to the problems they see in government.

Because of the confusion in government, and because of the bureaucracy, there is an inability to move decisively in foreign situations. We have lost more momentum in the foreign arms race than ever before. A military leader in a recent statement to Christian leaders in Washington, D.C. said there is no way that we can catch up with the Russians in arms development. He estimated that all the Russians will have to do in the near future is to say, "Move over; we are coming in." This is because of the comparatively archaic nature of our arms and our inability to defend ourselves and our allies. All around the world we don't have the capacity to respond. Communism has had one goal, and it has been proven historically—to take over the world. Our government does not believe that is possible. As a result, we are not prepared to react should it begin to take place.

The family is falling apart. Education is falling apart. Government is falling apart. And religion is falling apart.

Religion. We have an intense interest in religion today. People are interested in spiritual experiences, but such experiences have a broad range of expressions. Either they are humanistic, man-made religion on the one hand or on the other extreme, mysticism, such as the Hare Krishna movement. People seem to want to get away. Both attempts deal with the rampant problems they see in our society. In the United States we have two other extremes within Christian religion. One is liberalism, which includes the people who have said historically that they don't believe the Bible is the Word of God.

The other extreme is experience-oriented evangelicalism. Gallup Polls say that over 47 percent, or 50 million people, claim to have had a religious experience which might be termed "born again." Many people are coming to Christ all the time, but they are being attracted to the experience only and are not being grounded in the Scriptures.

Many young Christians seem to be getting their total training from Christian television shows. As good as Christian television may be, the content is not enough to build strong Christians. Because they are not related to God by either the Word of God or the Body of Christ, the Church, they are having a very minimal influence on their society.

These four institutions, the family, education, government, and religion are all on a rapid downward trend, perhaps the lowest point in history.

PHILOSOPHICAL DEGRADATION

If the first major problem is institutional, the second is philosophical. American society has lost the biblical world view it once had. America now has more of a humanistic or atheistic world view. A Jewish philosopher, Will Herbert, responded to this loss of our world view in an article called "Modern Man in the Metaphysical Wasteland." He wrote:

> The problem of the social order is a problem that in essence is theological and metaphysical. It is the theological and metaphysical tradition that has provided the sustaining armature of Western culture. . . . The underlying cause of this crisis is the fact that the spiritual armature of culture has reached an advanced state of disintegration. We are surrounded on all sides by the wreckage of our great intellectual tradition. In this kind of spiritual chaos, neither freedom nor order is possible. Instead of freedom, we live in the all ingulfing world of pleasure and power. Instead of order we have the jungle wilderness of normalness and self-indulgence. [Cited in *Save America*, H. Edward Rowe (Old Tappan, N.J.: Revell, 1976) p. 34]

No longer do people hold to moral or philosophical absolutes. They have said that there is no god of order. Humanism, the philosophy that says man can find the answers in himself, is very popular today. Narcissism, or self-love, is at a high point today. Situational ethics, which says to do whatever feels right for us, is common. The list goes on. All of them hold that there is no God, no moral base left in our culture. These philosophies are at the heart of the institutional demise.

Why do we have these problems? All of them relate in some way to the church and the body of Christ. Number one is the uninvolvement of the church today. Francis Schaeffer says that the church in the western world today is in a post-Christian era. There is very little influence by the church because we have failed to speak to the issues of our day and refused to deal with them. Hundreds of thousands of people are being massacred today in Cambodia and have been in recent years, but we as Christians have not dealt with this atrocity. Abortion is murder, but as Christians we have not dealt with that. Not only have we failed to deal with it academically, we have not even gotten angry about it. God wants us to get angry about the things that anger him. God has called us to deal with these issues biblically. We are to say, "This isn't right! That is wrong! There are absolutes! Life is sacred!" We are in a post-Christian era, where the Church has become idle. Edmund Burke said, "The only thing needed for evil to triumph is that good men do nothing," which is exactly what is happening in the Christian world today.

The second major reason for this philosophical degradation is the unawareness of the church. We are unaware of the issues. We need to be transformed by the renewing of our minds and not get our insights from the world. However, I do believe we need to be aware of the issues around us. We need to be aware of how humanism, atheism, materialism, narcissism, hedonism, and relativism are infiltrating every area of our thought lives and affecting our social order. Then we must deal with them from a biblical perspective.

Hitler came to a place of prominence in Germany when that country was at a socially, economically, and spiritually low ebb. Some of Hitler's greatest supporters were Christians because they were ignorant of the implications of Hitler's mentality as it related to Scripture. Paul wrote, "And this I pray, that your love may abound still more and more in real knowledge and all discernment, so that you may approve the things that are excellent, in order to be sincere and blameless until the day of Christ" (Phil. 1:9, 10).

God wants us to discern what comes out of our society today. He doesn't want us to look at every television show or go to every movie just because there is a cultural push or peer pressure, even by other Christians. He doesn't want us to read literature because other people are doing it. He doesn't want us to respond to political and social issues just because other people do. He wants us to think biblically. He wants us to grow in real knowledge and discernment in order that we might be able to say that this is of God and his kingdom or that is of Satan and the world.

The third major problem is that the Church, the body of Christ, is unhealthy. By and large, we have been lulled to sleep by Satan. Our senses have been so dulled that we have difficulty discerning right from wrong. Some of us are so sucked into the world system that we don't know what is happening around us. We read what is going on in the world today and it doesn't bother us at all.

It seems the resolution of the problem is twofold. There needs to be a revival and reawakening of the Church in America. We could be on the edge of that right now. God may be allowing us to see things happen like never before in America. England was at a low point at one time like us. John Wesley had such an impact on England that he aroused the people against the decay and decadence in government, business, and the church. Even though less than 2½ percent of the population was converted during Wesley's fifty-year ministry, the face of England was changed as that handful became like the salt of the earth. That small percentage was radically transformed by the reality of the Lordship of Christ. They lived the Christian life-style and dealt with issues in their society. Slave trade was stopped, four out of five taverns were closed for lack of business, prison and penal reforms were instituted, child labor laws were improved, and corruption in government declined. The list goes on. But the reason was a deep-rooted moral and spiritual awakening took place.

We need to see a reconstruction of societal influence. We need men and women at the top levels of society to be influencers for Christ—we need lawyers, educators, executives, and politicians who are being transformed by the power of Christ.

In addition, God wants men and women for full-time Christian ministry who will have an impact on the world outside the church. Jesus said we were to be like salt, to preserve the world as a permeating influence.

Success, as we have been discussing, has deep personal implications. We have responsibilities for making ourselves useful to God. No one can say he is successful as a person unless he is exerting an influence for Christ in the world around him. I believe that being successful today as a Christian means that we are to be salty.

ASSIGNMENT

1. In the light of this chapter, ask yourself whether you feel you and your church are part of the problem or part of the solution.

2. Seek some way of becoming involved in some type of impact on your society. Begin by sharing your faith with co-workers and with neighbors.

TEN
LIVING EACH DAY
SUCCESSFULLY

Life for us must have purpose. If we really want to find success, we must first determine what our purpose is and then have it become an integral part of our thinking. Five principles, if built into our life-style, can help us live in the light of our purpose.

God is going to hold us accountable one day for what we have done here on earth. If we have come to know Jesus Christ as Savior and Lord, we are going to be with him for eternity. But Christians don't just slide through life with no eternal or present consequences or rewards for how we live.

From the time Christ enters our lives to the time we go to be with the Lord could be minutes, hours, days, or years. It is during this time that God is going to hold us accountable for how well we have fulfilled his purpose. There are two things we are to major on in this life. In Matthew 6:33 we are told to seek first his kingdom and his righteousness and all these things shall be added unto us. The kingdom of God relates to the rule of Christ in the lives of men and women. So as we seek first his kingdom we are reaching people. When we seek first his righteousness, by the power of the Living Word, we are taking the written Word and building it into our lives. We are becoming righteous. We are growing in character.

Therefore, the two things all of us ought to work on all the time are to reach people in the most persuasive way possible and to build into ourselves the likeness of Christ as the Spirit of God works in us.

Those two things are important because they are the only two things over which we have control that will have eternal consequences. So, whatever we do to influence people or the Word of God as it relates to us will last forever and have eternal results. We build a capacity in this life to glorify God throughout all eternity. Scripture talks about crowns that we will one day receive. Crowns represent authority. Believers will have positions of authority in eternity based upon their faithfulness to the fulfillment of God's purpose for them in this life. Some people will have a higher reigning position from which they will glorify God throughout eternity. The position is going to be contingent upon how they lived in this life.

In the light of this, there are five things we can do that will help us accomplish God's purpose for us.

SEE OUR PURPOSE CLEARLY

In order to see our purpose, we first need to have specific goals and objectives related to our lives. We always ought to be working on specific things.

Second, we need to be single-minded in our approach. Paul said this one thing I do, not these forty things I dabble in. Paul was single-minded. He wrote: "Do you not know that those who run in a race all run, but only one receives the prize? Run in such a way that you may win" (1 Cor. 9:24). We are running toward a specific prize. He wrote: "And everyone who competes in the games exercises self-control in all things" (v. 25a). We must bring everything in control of our body to achieve the objective. He wrote: "They then do it to receive a perishable wreath, but we an imperishable. Therefore I run in such a way, as not without aim; I box in such a way, as not beating the air; but I buffet my body and I make it my slave, lest possibly, after I have preached to others, I myself should be disqualified" (vv. 25-27). He didn't want to be disqualified from effectiveness in this life or from the benefits of eternal life.

Paul said, "I buffet my body." That comes from the metaphor of boxing and the Greek games. Paul literally meant, "I beat my body black and blue. I bring everything in my life under control in order that I might win the race. I run in order that I might win."

Jack Hyles, pastor of one of the largest churches in America, once shared an illustration of single-mindedness. At a Christian college there was a guy named Joe, who had a harelip. His friends were often making fun of him. Joe used to go around campus saying, "I'm going to be a 'pwreather.' " The guys used to say, "You're going to be a 'pwreather,' Joe?"

Then one day the most beautiful girl on campus walked by. No one would ask her out because she was so gorgeous. Joe was with the guys and said, "I'm gonna mawwy her." They ran over to her and told her that Joe said he was going to marry her. She just smiled politely and walked off.

Joe had a vision, a purpose, a goal. He went back to his room and got in front of the mirror and started practicing, "Will you go out with me? Will you go out with me?" Finally he had it down perfectly. He ran across campus, entered the girl's dorm, invited the girl downstairs and asked, "Will you go out with me?"

She answered, "Joe! Did you practice and practice just for me?"

He said, "I thur did!" They went out, and they did later get married! And Joe did become a great preacher! Why? Because he was single-minded. Great people are people who try just a bit harder than average people. They don't quit, because they are single-minded. Unless we are single-minded, and know where we are going, and know why God has called us, and live in the light of it, we'll never achieve it.

WANT IT DESPERATELY

The desire for purpose in life is one of the missing elements in the church and in Christendom today. "Blessed are those who hunger and thirst after righteousness, for they shall be satisfied" (Matt. 5:6). We must hunger and thirst after it. Seek first the kingdom of God. Search for wisdom the way we search for silver and gold.

Socrates was walking by the water one day when a young man came up to him and said, "Socrates, may I be your disciple?" Socrates didn't answer, but started wading out into the water. The young man followed, asking the same question over and over.

When Socrates reached the place where the water was about chest deep, he turned on the young man, grabbed him by the top of his head and pushed him under the water and held him there until he knew he could take it no more. The young man came up gasping for air. Socrates said, "Young man, when you desire truth as much as you desire air, then you can be my disciple."

I think God would say that to us today. We may be saying, "God use me!"

And God would ask us, "How much do you want to be used? Do you want it desperately?" So often we neutralize our feelings. We don't become people of great passion. We ought to hate sin with the greatest passion. But we must have a passion for the things that God wants us to have a passion for if we are to be used as he would like to use us.

We must realize the eternal importance of all that we do. Paul wrote: "But we have his treasure in earthen vessels, that the surpassing greatness of the power may be of God and not from ourselves; we are afflicted in every way, but not crushed; perplexed, but not despairing; persecuted, but not forsaken; struck down, but not destroyed; always carrying about in the body the dying of Jesus, that the life of Jesus also may be manifested in our body. For we who live are constantly being delivered over to death for Jesus' sake, that the life of Jesus also may be manifested in our mortal flesh" (2 Cor. 4:7-11). He was going through all that affliction. Yet he wrote: "Therefore we do not lose heart, but though our outer man is decaying, yet our inner man is being renewed day by day. For momentary, light affliction is producing for us an eternal weight of glory far beyond all comparison, while we look not at the things which are seen, but at the things which are not seen; for the things which are seen are temporal, but the things which are not seen are eternal" (2 Cor. 4:6-18).

Paul knew that everything he did, all the suffering he went through, was nothing compared to the eternal weight of glory that he was going to receive. He had a great passion because he knew the eternal implications and importance of all that he did. We must have that if we are going to want something desperately.

"As a man thinks in his heart, so is he." We ought to have a purpose and goals and keep them before us and think about them frequently. We should pray about them, that God will build those principles into our lives. We need also to tell others about our purpose.

I recently became the president of the International School of Theology. I told a number of people that, "Either we are going to reach our objectives or else I'm going to die in the process, or be fired. Those are the only alternatives. I'm not going to quit." When I verbalized that it really put credibility on the line. There was no turning back. We need to commit ourselves to our purpose and tell people about it and not turn from it.

Years ago, when Cortez wanted to conquer Mexico, his seven ships dropped anchor off the shores. When all the men were ashore, they smelled something burning. As they turned around, they saw their ships being burned up. Then Cortez said, "I did that on purpose because there are only two alternatives. Now we either win or die, but there is no turning back." That is what God wants—that desperate, "I've got to do it or I'm going to die in the process. It is God's purpose and he placed me here to fulfill it. I've got to live in light of it."

ACCOMPLISH IT ENTHUSIASTICALLY

Dr. Charles Spurgeon was once asked by a young man, "How can I get people to come hear me preach like people come to hear you preach?" He answered "Just douse yourself with kerosene and set yourself afire and they'll come and watch you burn." It is a good principle. If we are on fire, people are attracted to us. If we are enthusiastic, people will want to be around us.

Recently, in one of the seminaries a young man who had finished his senior preaching assignment went up to his professor and said, "Prof, what would be an appropriate prayer to close the sermon with?"

The professor said, "Now I lay me down to sleep. . . ."

There is a lack of enthusiasm and power in many of our pulpits today. It might be true in our lives as well. People are attracted to people who are sold out for something. If we are not enthusiastic about Christ, people are going to be attracted to cults or others that are enthusiastic about what they are doing.

Scripture says, "Whatever you do, do your work heartily as for the Lord rather than for men" (Col. 3:23). Since the word "enthusiasm" comes from the Greek words *en theos* (in God), for a person to be "in God" and not enthused is a contradiction of terms.

FOLLOW IT FAITHFULLY

One of the best illustrations of following one's purpose faithfully is found in 2 Corinthians 11:24-29:

> Five times I received from the Jews thirty-nine lashes. Three times I was beaten with rods, once I was stoned, three times I was shipwrecked, a night and a day I have spent in the deep. I have been on frequent journeys, in dangers from rivers, dangers from robbers, dangers from my countrymen, dangers from the Gentiles, dangers in the city, dangers in the wilderness, dangers on the sea, dangers among false brethren; I have been in labor and hardship, through many sleepless nights, in hunger and thirst, often without food, in cold and exposure. Apart from such external things, there is the daily pressure upon me of

114

concern for all the churches. Who is weak without my being weak? Who is led into sin without my intense corcern?

Those externals were essentially meaningless to Paul because he had such a passion for the internals—what was happening in the lives of people. Because he loved people so much, because he loved God so much, the outward pains were nothing.

Compare yourself with what this man went through and ask yourself how you rate compared to him:

> In 1831, failed in business; 1832, defeated for legislature; 1833 again failed in business; 1834, elected to legislature; 1835, a sweetheart died; 1836, had a nervous breakdown; 1838, defeated for legislative speaker; 1840, defeated for elector; 1843, defeated for Congress; 1846, elected to Congress; 1848, defeated for Congress; 1855, defeated for Senate; 1856, defeated for vice president; 1858, defeated for Senate."

When would you have quit? Well, he didn't quit. That is why in 1860 he became known as President Abraham Lincoln.

General Patton was a man who just didn't quit. During the war, with devastation all around him, and death, blood, brutality in front of him, to the side, and behind him, one of his lieutenants overheard him say, "God, I love it!"

Some may think that was perverted, but it wasn't necessarily. From his perspective it may have been—but not for us, for we don't struggle against flesh and blood. We do struggle against principalities and powers. The Christian life is filled with conflict all the time. God wants us to say that though there is death in front of us, people around us are frustrated, defeated. We're getting persecuted; we're a minority; and it seems there is no way to win the battle. That's the time we ought to be able to say, "God, I love it. I love it because I'm right where you want me to be, doing exactly what you want me to do. I thank you because you always lead me in your victory in Christ I'm always successful." He doesn't want quitters; he wants people who will keep going forward.

REVIEW, REALIGN, AND REDEDICATE YOURSELF REGULARLY

We should stop every day and ask: "God, am I doing it? Am I reaching your goals for me?" The important thing isn't that we always reach the specific objectives that we set. It is very hard to get specific, black and white, God-inspired biblical objectives. They are but a means to an end. But we should keep pressing toward the purpose for which God has called us. Even if we fail in the process, so what? We are going to fail. God doesn't want us to fail all the time as a way of life, but if we do fail, we should stop and reevaluate what went wrong, rededicate ourselves, and realign ourselves and move on toward where we need to be.

If we can build these five principles into our lives, we will be able to pray as Paul prayed when he knew that his time on earth was about ready to be eclipsed. He knew he was going to go home to be with the Lord. "I am already being poured out as a drink offering, and the time of my departure has come. I have fought the good fight, I have finished the course, I have kept the faith." He was saying that he had done everything that he could to accomplish what God wanted him to do.

Wouldn't we like to be able to say that? "God I've finished your course for me. I know that in the future there is laid up for me the crown of righteousness." I pray that we will be able to say that—that we will get the burden to live in the light of the purpose for which God put us here.

ASSIGNMENT
1. Practice these five principles of success daily by meditating on them four times a day for ten to twenty minutes each time.
2. Keep a daily log of the progress you see.
3. Have Christian friends keep you accountable for the specific goals you set for yourself.